IN SEARCH OF CANADA
The Early Years of John Wesley Dafoe

IN SEARCH OF CANADA
THE EARLY YEARS OF JOHN WESLEY DAFOE

CHRISTOPHER DAFOE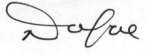

GREAT PLAINS
PUBLICATIONS

Great Plains Publications
233 Garfield Street S
Winnipeg, MB R3G 2M1
www.greatplains.mb.ca

Great Plains Publications gratefully acknowledges the financial support provided for its publishing program by the Government of Canada through the Canada Book Fund; the Canada Council for the Arts; the Province of Manitoba through the Book Publishing Tax Credit and the Book Publisher Marketing Assistance Program; and the Manitoba Arts Council.

Design & Typography by Relish New Brand Experience
Printed in Canada by Friesens

LIBRARY AND ARCHIVES CANADA CATALOGUING IN PUBLICATION

Dafoe, Christopher, author
          In search of Canada : the early years of John Wesley Dafoe / Christopher Dafoe.

Includes bibliographical references and index.
ISBN 978-1-926531-94-6 (pbk.)

          1. Dafoe, John W., 1866-1944. 2. Newspaper editors--Canada--Biography. 3. Journalists--Canada--Biography. 4. Newspaper publishing--Canada--History. 5. Winnipeg Free Press--Biography. 6. Canada--Politics and government--20th century. I. Title.

PN4913.D3D34 2014   070.92   C2013-908543-2

ENVIRONMENTAL BENEFITS STATEMENT

Great Plains Publications saved the following resources by printing the pages of this book on chlorine free paper made with 100% post-consumer waste.

TREES	WATER	ENERGY	SOLID WASTE	GREENHOUSE GASES
8	3,770	4	253	695
FULLY GROWN	GALLONS	MILLION BTUs	POUNDS	POUNDS

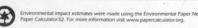

Environmental impact estimates were made using the Environmental Paper Network Paper Calculator 3.2. For more information visit www.papercalculator.org.

FSC
www.fsc.org
MIXTE
Papier issu
de sources
responsables
FSC® C016245

Contents

Ponemah, Summer 1939

As the 1930s came to a close, John Wesley Dafoe, editor of the *Winnipeg Free Press* since 1901, was widely regarded at home and abroad as the foremost Canadian journalist of his time. A few called him the greatest Canadian of his generation. Born poor in the backwoods of Canada West in 1866, a newspaperman since 1883, he had served on the Canadian delegation to the Versailles peace conference in 1919, lectured at Oxford, helped establish the Canadian Press news service, turned down a knighthood, published numerous books including celebrated studies of Wilfrid Laurier and Clifford Sifton and had been since 1930 Chancellor of the University of Manitoba and a Fellow of the Royal Society of Canada since 1926. In August 1937 he had been named a member of the Royal Commission on Dominion-Provincial Relations—the Rowell-Sirois Commission—travelling extensively by air and rail to all parts of the Dominion.

By mid-July 1939 he was 73 and feeling it. His family hoped that he would slow down, but with a world war looming retirement seemed out of the question. The memoir he planned to write in the cabin his brother Cal had built for him in a corner of the family compound at Ponemah on the west shore of Lake Winnipeg would have to wait. He knew that running an editorial page in wartime would be as taxing as the long struggle through the thirties when his had been one of the few and unpopular voices raised against the policy of appeasing Hitler, but he had always liked a good fight and he was ready for one more, old age be damned.

In the meantime, while waiting for hostilities to begin, he was intent on finishing his work on the Rowell-Sirois Report for the royal commission. In a letter written from Ponemah on 27 July to his daughter Elizabeth, he chatted about the world situation and how he expected the November meeting in Victoria of the Institute for Pacific Relations to be wrecked by the Japanese. He then went on to describe the hectic activity in Ottawa and elsewhere where Commission members and staff were struggling to get the report together and published "in both languages" by 12 October. In fact, it would be May 1940 before the final report was handed in to Ottawa and the nine provinces, with the nation on a war footing and domestic matters more or less in the shade for the foreseeable future.

On that summer day in 1939, however, he was basking on the verandah and planning some work on the Report. "I brought some papers along," he wrote, "thinking I might get an hour's quiet to work at them. I sat me down on the verandah of the cabin; there are now assembled in the room Michael, Peter, John and Kit, David Dawson and Dickie Elsey. They are discussing putting on a dramatic performance on Saturday (swift workers these boys) but they are not agreed on what to produce—Snow White and the Seven Dwarfs appears to have the inside track. Kit is playing the mouth organ. Somehow I don't think I'll do much work here."

It was, sadly, an accurate prediction. His grandsons and their friends settled for a circus and by the end of summer there was no time to look back. The planned memoirs were abandoned until the return of peace and the hoped for retirement to the cabin at Ponemah. He died suddenly in Winnipeg on a cold Sunday in early January 1944.

That unwritten memoir would have told a particularly Canadian story, the tale of a young man of humble background and unexpected talents making good in nineteenth century fashion in a country that was just beginning to find its way in a changing world. That he never lived to tell the whole story is unfortunate because his personal memories never faded and he knew most of the Canadian story and the principal players of those years at first hand. But memory lives on in other ways. As part of his family legacy, John Dafoe left hundreds of letters, written by himself and others, that offer another way of entry into the past. At various periods in his life he wrote brief accounts of his early career, for use on public occasions or on radio broadcasts. He lived on, as well, in the memories of his children and the grandchildren of his old age. This archive of memory gives us a candid glimpse of that lost Canada and the story of his remarkable early years as he might have told it himself if he had not been prevented by a busy life and an old age cut short.

I was almost eight years old when my grandfather died and I have carried many vivid memories of him through the years. The kindly, popular backwoods school teacher of the 1880s lived on in the old political warrior of the 1930s and 1940s. His own childhood had been austere, but he always had time for children, cancelling an important editorial meeting in order to take the cousins to the circus, stopping by at our house after a long day at his desk to drop off a book or a large string bag of mandarin oranges or to chat about school days, his and ours. There were interesting restaurant lunches and walks down Portage Avenue when I was amazed to see how many passersby seemed to know him, greeting him by name.

Closely engaged in contemporary politics, issues and literature, he was, to a child as young as I was then, a curiously old-fashioned figure, a Victorian gentleman, like a character you might discover in a good book, a larger-than-life Merlin figure who wore pince-nez with a string hanging down and laced boots. He took you on his knee and read you spellbinding stories by writers such as S.R. Crockett, Jefferey Farnol and E. Nesbit. He owned a top hat and carried a walking stick.

He had a small grandstand constructed on his front lawn so that family, friends and neighbours could watch the King and

Queen drive by in an open car one chilly day in May, 1939. Photos taken on the day indicate that he was not present for the occasion, having been summoned to Ottawa to take part in ceremonies there.

There was a typewriter in the study at his big house on Wellington Crescent, but he never touched it, leaving such gadgetry to trained stenographers, modern novelists and young newsmen with a taste for the new-fangled. We later used it to produce a little in-house newspaper at the cottage. He did all his writing with a fat yellow copy pencil or a fountain pen, leaving others to set it in type or process it on the Underwood for dispatch to his publishers or to the university journal that had requested it.

At one point in the late twenties or early thirties he attempted to learn to drive a car, managing to put it through a shop window before agreeing with his instructor that it would be best to leave the driving to others. The *Free Press* provided a car and chauffeur to convey him around Winnipeg.

In the 1940s, in an attempt to promote gasoline conservation in wartime, he took to riding to and from his office in an open landau in fine weather and when, one early morning, I appeared standing alone at the end of our street he stopped the carriage and let me climb up beside the driver for a ride downtown. I spent a glorious Saturday morning at the *Free Press*, having my name set in hot type, running up and down the spiral staircase that led to the composing room, getting an advance look at next week's coloured comics and generally getting in the way. I also met the compositor who had the daunting task of deciphering my grandfather's hand-written articles.

Like other members of my family, I had the habit, when I was a small boy, of turning up, unannounced, at grandpa's house and hanging around until I was invited to stay for dinner; children had freedom to wander in those days. I particularly liked to present myself on a Saturday afternoon when grandpa, back

from lunch with his pals at the Manitoba Club—a group known
to outsiders as the "Sanhedrin" and to grandpa as "The Black
Hand Gang"—might be available for a chat or possibly a ramble
down by the Assiniboine River, which passed by at the bottom of
the garden. At dinner the issues of the day were hotly debated by
the grownups over the roast beef and an attentive child could be
privy to fascinating inside information about Mackenzie King or
Mr. Churchill. On one never-to-be-forgotten occasion during an
unusual lull in the conversation, grandpa turned to me and whis-
pered "And what do you think Kit?"

Now I am close to the age that grandpa had reached when
I saw him for the last time. Reading his letters of the 1880s and
1890s when I was preparing to start work on this evocation of
his early years I suddenly realized with a pang that I was the old
man now and that he was forever young in the pages of the letters I was trying so hard to decipher. It is a young man's story that
I found in those letters; it is his story. I am only the compositor.

His status as a public figure has been evaluated in three bi-
ographies, by a colleague, George Ferguson, and by historians
Murray Donnelly and Ramsay Cook as well as in numerous academic studies and articles. This is not an academic study of the
life and work of John Wesley Dafoe. This is the story of the man
his family and his friends knew, from his unpromising beginnings
in the backwoods of pre-Confederation Ontario to his early and
unexpected success in nineteenth-century Canadian journalism;
his background, his education, his early career, the establishment
of his family, his rise as a national and international figure and
his lifelong search for a true Canadian identity. Some of it is told
in his own words, some is drawn from the recollections of those
who knew him. It is a quintessentially Canadian story and one
that is worth remembering.

Christopher Dafoe
Ponemah, Summer 2012

THE PALATINES

"There is no doubt about it that our forefathers were Dutch," John Wesley Dafoe wrote to a distant cousin in 1933. "I am told that my grandfather could speak Dutch, although English was his language, and Isaiah Dafoe, who belongs to the Cornwall branch of the family, told me that his grandmother and grandfather invariably talked Dutch to one another. This rather tells against the theory that the founder of the family was a Walloon and therefore French speaking..."

Confusion about Dafoe family origins persisted through much of the twentieth century, a perplexing problem at census time when confronting the notorious census question about "racial origin." One Dafoe aunt insisted on claiming Canadian origin, pointing out that the family had been here long enough, although she expected to be arrested and possibly jailed by the census authorities for doing so.

Modern genealogical research rejects both the Dutch and the Walloon connections, tracing the family to one Daniel Thevou, born in Switzerland, possibly in the village of Missy near Geneva in 1665. A similar name, "Thevoz," is said to occur today in the Canton of Vaud and records show that in the seventeenth century it was sometimes spelled "Thevou."

Daniel Thevou, an agricultural labourer, worked as a vine dresser and sometime around 1700 he and his wife Marianne—nee Delcour—migrated in search of work to the wine country of south Germany, a region that had seen its population much reduced during the past century in wars between Catholics and Protestants. Daniel, a Calvinist who appears to have been a German speaker, settled in Germany in time to be a victim of one of the greatest natural disasters to strike southern Germany in the eighteenth century. The hard winter of 1708-09 killed the vines and put thousands out of work. Faced with starvation and religious persecution, the Thevous joined a British resettlement scheme—the Palatine Migration—that took thousands of victims of the agricultural disaster out of Germany via the Rhine and Holland for resettlement in Ireland and North America. The Thevou family, members of the Reformed Church, are said to have been assisted by Mennonites and Anabaptists during the difficult passage through country torn by religious strife, reaching the port of Rotterdam after a journey lasting several weeks. They were then loaded on a ship bound for London.

The Thevous, with two children, arrived in London in late summer 1709 and, with thousands of other migrants, lived in tents on Blackheath or possibly at Deptford until January 1710 when the group destined for North America was packed into ships to make ready for the nine-week voyage to New York. Long delays followed and the ships did not sail until April. By the time they reached New York they had been on board ship for six months. But the nightmare was far worse than that. As the Thevous' ship left Portsmouth typhus broke out on board. Marianne Thevou was among those who died.

The surviving members of the family, Daniel and his daughter Marianna, 10, and his son Abraham, 7, were settled first near the new village of Beckmansland, near present day Rhinebeck, where Daniel soon married Marie Barbara Krass, the widow of a fellow Palatine, and where the children grew up speaking German, the "Dutch" or "Deutsch" that some of their descendants recalled hearing about.

It is easy to see how later generations became confused about family origins. There is clearly Swiss/French in the deep background with a later overlay of German. In Beckmansland the Thevous were surrounded by German neighbours, but there were also many English-speaking settlers along the Hudson as well as a large contingent of Dutch speakers from the old colony. With the passage of time, the family name, originally pronounced "Tay-vuh" became "Day-fuh" and, in time, the name assumed a variety of forms, such as "Deffu," "Defou," "Diefuh," and "Devoe," possibly as a result of confused interpretation by English- or Dutch-speaking neighbours, who only heard the name spoken, never saw it written down. We know nothing of the educational attainments of those early family members and it is entirely possible that some or many of them signed with a cross. Later in the century, some of the grandchildren of Daniel were calling themselves "Dafoe," with the accent on the first syllable, just where their Swiss ancestors had placed it—Day-foe.

Records show that Daniel Thevou and his son Abraham were naturalized as British subjects at Kingston, New York, in September 1715, the last time that the spelling "Thevou" appears on an official document. Two years later Daniel died, probably at Germantown, New York, leaving his young children to face the future with a step-mother. Within a few years both were married and producing large families. Marianna had six children and Abraham at least eight. The Thevous were becoming a North American family, but under a slightly different name. Abraham, who called himself "Devoe," farmed near Rhinebeck, dying there in 1753. In 1724 he had married Anna Maria Catharina Reiffenberger, also a Palatine, producing five sons and three daughters of whom records have been found. The eldest, born circa 1725, was "Johannes" or "John" Ernst, known in his youth as "Defuh," but who came, in time, to be called "John Defoe," possibly as a result of living among English speakers, some of whom may have had a certain familiarity with English literature.

John Ernst married Mary Keller, also a German-speaking Palatine (two of her sisters also married sons of Abraham), at Germantown Reformed Church in February 1749. They were soon running a grist mill near Petersburg in the Hoosick River area. When illness broke out at Petersburg, John and Mary moved the family, "overnight" as it is recorded, to Washtub Creek near Pownal, "just over the mountain." Here John re-established his mill, cleared a farm and planted an orchard. He was elected Pathmaster at Pownal in 1768 and Deer Reeve in 1769-1770. The family continued to grow and by 1769 there were eight children, seven boys and a girl. The Defoes might have lived out their lives at Pownal, watching their family grow from generation to generation, but History was on the march. Their stable world was about to collapse around them.

For much of the eighteenth century the family had lived in or close to the old Van Rensselaer "patroonship" in the upper Hudson Valley. "Van Rensselaer" was an important name to settlers in the region and it is not surprising that over the generations, down to the present time, the name has cropped up on the Dafoe family tree. An old family legend has it that at some point in the misty past a Dafoe married into the patroon family—possibly there was an elopement. No evidence exists for this romantic claim and it seems likely that the name was co-opted to add a hint of aristocratic glamour to an otherwise humble colonial family that had hopes of rising in a changing world.

The Revolutionary War divided the descendants of Daniel Thevou. Some attempted, not always successfully, to remain aloof from the conflict raging around them. At least one son of Abraham Devoe served in the Continental Army. John Ernst Defoe and his family, for reasons that have not been recorded, opted for the Loyalist or "Tory" side. Perhaps they were conscious of their debt to the British crown which had provided a home for them in America. We know that John Ernst was among the Loyalists rounded up and jailed in 1776 and that, as one of his sons later recalled, he broke out in 1777 after learning that he and others were about to be shot "and went into Burgoyne's camp, and very shortly after fought in the battle of Bennington where he was unfortunately taken prisoner and put into close confinement and irons, which situation he suffered for nearly twelve months." Then he escaped for the second time.

Bennington, which was more of a skirmish than a battle, nevertheless had a profound effect upon the family. Three of John's sons—Abraham, Conrad and George—also participated in the action and George was among those killed. John and his sons were now firmly involved in the Loyalist cause. John Ernst's sons John, Abraham, Jacob, Michael and Daniel, served with the King's Rangers under Lt. Col. Robert Rogers, although Daniel, who was only 14 in 1783, must have seen little or no action. Another son, Conrad, was in the King's Royal Regiment of New York, while John Ernst himself lived dangerously as a courier and spy for the British, attached to Rogers' Rangers and maintaining communications between Crown Point and the British garrison at New York. According to some accounts, "Old John" took his family under a flag of truce "out of the land of Rebellion" to Fort St. John's (present day St. Jean-sur-Richelieu, Quebec) in the summer of 1781, shortly before the surrender of Cornwallis at Yorktown on 19 October. This party appears to have consisted of Old John's wife Mary, his daughter Mary, the younger sons Michael and Daniel, who soon rallied to the colours, and his sister Eva Katzebach, who later settled at Sorel, remaining there until her death. On Christmas Eve, 1783, the sons of John Ernst as well as Andrew Rikley, husband of their sister Mary, were mustered out of the royal service at St. John's, Quebec. Plans were already afoot to resettle them farther along the St. Lawrence, deeper into the wilderness that would, in time, become the province of Upper Canada. Old John, however, was not to join the remnants of his family on the bateaux that would take them along the river to the Promised Land. One day between the spring and summer of 1784 he died at St. John's, possibly of malaria contracted during his years of arduous service to the lost cause.

Members of John Ernst's family are listed as both "Dafoe" and "Defoe" in the "Old U.E. List" published in 1885 to commemorate the loyalist centennial celebrations of 1884, indicating some confusion among the clerks who made up the original lists in 1784. A document of 1788 survives in which Mary, the widow of John Ernst, signs her name "Defoe," while her sons Conrad, Michael, Abraham and "Dannel" opt for "Dafoe." The latter spelling, however, appears to have been firmly established by the time family members took up lands at their new home near Fredericksburgh and Adolphustown on the Bay of Quinte.

There is little to tell of Daniel, the youngest Dafoe son. We know that he was born at Hoosick, New York province on 13 September 1769 and that he may have served briefly in the Loyalist forces at the end of the Revolutionary war. We know that he married Elizabeth Wright at Fredericksburgh in 1786 and that records show that he contributed two pounds to the building fund of a new Methodist church at Hay Bay in 1792. He was a farmer all his life and died at Fredericksburg in 1842. His family was large, consisting of 11 children. His third son, Samuel, was born in 1797 and later farmed at Zion's Hill, Thurlow Township, where he and his wife Eve Wright raised seven children, one of whom, Calvin, born in 1841, became the father of John Wesley Dafoe.

Two of Samuel Dafoe's sons became doctors, but Cal, true to the traditions of his European ancestors, stayed on the farm. In October 1861 he married Mary Elcome, late of Kent, England, who had arrived in the settlement with her widowed father John Elcome in 1857. The young couple lived and worked on Samuel Dafoe's farm for the first few years of their marriage, but in the spring of 1865 Cal and Mary, with two young children, William and Margaret, followed John Elcome up the Hastings road to newly opened lands about 120 miles north-west of Belleville in Bangor Township, North Hastings county. A house was raised on the rocky soil across the Peterson Road from John Elcome's land a few miles from the rising village of Combermere across the line in Renfrew County and there on 8 March 1866 John Wesley Dafoe was born.

So it was that the descendants of Daniel Thevou, like many North American families of long standing, became, at last, a family of mixed heritage with a new name, coined in the New World. By the beginning of the twenty-first century there were thousands of them, living in all parts of North America.

COMBERMERE

Calvin Dafoe stood to inherit his father's farm at Zion's Hill. He was already making a name for himself in the district as a school trustee and master of the local Orange Lodge, but father Samuel had taken out loans to finance the medical training of two of his other sons and Cal could expect to acquire a heavy mortgage along with the land. It must have seemed to him more reasonable to take up land of his own in the newly opened district to the north. Mary would be near her father who had already made the journey and Cal would feel, for the first time that he was his own master. So the journey was made, the task of land-clearing begun and their first, rough dwelling constructed. There in 1866, a year after their arrival, a third child was born. He was christened John Wesley, a reflection of his English mother's non-conformist roots. She would always call him John, but to the family, to the woman who became his wife and to the troops of friends he recruited along the way during his long and busy life he would be, always and forever, "Jack."

Looking back a few weeks before his death in 1944, Dafoe would say: "In the successes which have come to me I know that fortune played a large part. When I think of the young men that I started life with and recall what happened to some of them, I realize that the race is not always to the swift nor the battle to the strong. I was born under a favourable star." There was no discernable gleam of that "favourable star" in the year 1866 or for many years afterwards.

"I was born tongue-tied," he recalled in later life, "and had to be operated on several times before I got the partial use of my tongue, although it was not until I was 10 or 12 that I could speak plainly. One of these operations took place when I was about 2 years old and my sister Maggie witnessed it with much interest. A day or so later mother left us together and went out doors. Maggie at once suggested that she should continue the operation with a case knife and I agreed. When mother arrived on the scene a moment or two later I was blood from head to foot and my mouth was cut pretty much from ear to ear." The botched operation had no adverse effect on his regard for his elder sister. Years later he would write: "I think Maggie is dearer to me than any of my brothers and sisters. I guess it is the memory of thousands of days we spent together in the old and far off childish days and many and many scrapes we got into together. I always think of Maggie as she was in girlish days, quick-tempered, impulsive. Wayward at times, but with a heart as true and tender as ever beat in human breast."

Deprived of unhampered vocal expression, young Jack may have begun to develop an active inner life sooner than other children. From his earliest years he was introspective, dreamy and inclined to wander in the woods around the farm. As he grew older he was seen to be bookish and disinclined to participate enthusiastically in the chores that were assigned to farm children. At haymaking time he was sent to the barn to receive loads of hay, loafing about with a book or "old civil war days copies of *Harper's* magazine" between loads "until the tramp of the horses on the barn floor told me that my holiday was over. In those days I would read anything. There was nothing too abstruse for me to tackle even though I could not understand it." Lazy days were soon only a memory, however. "Next year they thought I was big enough to be of some service in the field so I had to go out and follow the wagon with a rake gathering up the leavings."

Cal was not pleased to see his son with a book in his hands. "When I was a very little lad," Jack recalled, "owing to my dislike for humdrum farm work, my people came to the conclusion that I was good for nothing—all except my mother who had faith in me and induced my father to send me to friends where I could go to school."

"My earliest recollection," he wrote in his twenties, "is of sitting up in a highchair watching an aunt of mine get married. I remember the scene distinctly although it appears from the date that I was only about two months old at the time." Possibly more reliable is his memory of another wedding held in the Dafoe farm house when he was seven: "I remember it distinctly too, for I kept raiding the pantry for cookies and other delicacies until the servant found me in the act of demolishing a pie around the corner of the house and we had a lively interview. I can unhesitatingly assert that she had a very strong arm."

Cal found much to deplore in his second son, but when Jack was a child his father, who despaired of ever getting any work out of this bookish boy, was delighted to detect a tendency toward political zeal uncommon in one so young. Combermere in the 1870s was, like the rest of Ontario, a hot-bed of Orangeism. The Dafoes were hard-boned Tories and in that era membership in the local Orange Lodge was, more often than not, part and parcel of membership in the Conservative Party. "In our country," Jack recalled, "the 12th of July was the biggest day of the year and as we were flanked by two Irish settlements, Maynooth and Bridewell, there were very often little unpleasantnesses on that day. When I was about 10 years old I was a great Orangeman."

He could sing, "in the approved style," such provocative songs as "Croppy Lie Down," "Boyne Water," and "The Protestant Boys." "The words have gone from me, but the airs linger in my head yet. I remember I used to be able to beat them on the drums although I never could master the shrill music of the fife. My father, a staunch

Orangeman although he had not a drop of Irish blood in him, was very proud of me. He used to tell my brother Will who would not join either the Young Britons or the Orangemen that when I grew up he would have one son an Orangeman. Alas for his hopes. In some respects I have disappointed my parents. My father expected me to be a Tory and an Orangeman; my mother had hopes that I would develop into a Methodist minister. And I am instead a Radical in politics, a despiser of the Orangemen taken collectively and neither a minister nor a Methodist. And in other ways I have also disappointed them, for father used to say that I would never earn enough to buy salt for ink. In this he was a little mistaken."

Writing to his future wife in 1889, he assured her that "You need not be afraid of my family. They are not at all ferocious. They are only simple country folks who know little of the world and its conventionalities, but who have what is perhaps better— kindly hearts under a somewhat rough exterior."

Nevertheless, he could look back years later and marvel at the narrowness of the home life he had lived as a child in Combermere. "It seemed to me that in their unsparing condem- nation of all the graces and arts they were taking from life many of the things that make it endurable. My mother has broadened into a liberal-minded woman. When I was a little fellow she was still a young woman who was trying to live up to the tenets of a narrow creed. I have a very keen remembrance of those years. The books in our house were limited to the Methodist Hymn Book, the Bible, the Methodist *Book of Discipline*; the *Christian Guardian* and the local paper completed our supply of reading material. No novel ever found its way into the house; no songs were ever sung except in our wayward moments when we were out in the barn, and Sunday was one long agony."

Jack's early exposure to backwoods Methodism may help to explain his lifelong ambivalence in matters of religion. As a young man he would write: "Probably as a punishment on my parents for calling me John Wesley, I soured on the Methodist Church a good many years ago. Mainly I think on account of the ignorant, intolerant, officious busybodies they used to send as itinerant missionaries on the backwoods circuits. My soul used to rise up in arms against them with their uncouth manners, atrocious habits of speech and dogmatic utterances on all subjects. We occasionally got visits from an English church clergyman to whom I took a strong liking; he was so broad-minded, tolerant, gentle and refined. He was the Reverend R.D. Mills of Eganville, a strong friend of Mr. MacKay's [also an Anglican cleric]. I remember the Methodist missionaries and their satellites used to have an idea, to which they frequently gave utterance, that in some way Mr. Mills and Mr. MacKay were in league with the evil one, because they did not denounce from their pulpits such heinous crimes as dancing, etc. There was a gathering once upon a time which Mr. and Mrs. Mills attended. They even tarried to see the dancing of the young men and maidens under the tall maples. The settlement was scandalized for weeks afterwards."

The Dafoe homestead, a clearing on a steep hillside, hardly qualified as a farm. "The country," Jack's younger sister Edith recalled almost a lifetime later, "was rich in scenery, if nothing else." To help make ends meet, Cal Dafoe spent winters working in the lumber camps, returning at the end of the spring drive to resume his struggle with the land. Life was hard and dangerous for everybody. Once a wildcat came down the chimney and once, when Cal was away, Mary had to face down a drunken stranger who walked into the house while the family was eating dinner. "Roads," Edith remembered, "were dangerous for children. Clearings with small houses were scattered along the road, but in between was the inevitable bush. Wild animals were common, principally bears, but also wolves and wolverines."

There is a family legend that Cal was at one time in his youth a notorious bar-room brawler. He stood close to six foot eight inches tall in his boots and it was said that he would on occasion bring a large fist down on the bar and shout "I'm Cal Dafoe and I can lick any son of a bitch in the house!" Another family legend—one shared with many other families with a backwoods background—has it that his drinking and brawling days came to an abrupt end one night when he turned after uttering his challenge and found himself confronting "God's Messenger," an angel with a fiery sword. His salad days over, he became a sober family man, hard working and an example to his neighbours, although hot-tempered and impetuous.

"I could not begin to give you an idea of my father," he told his wife-to-be in 1889. "It is only of late years that I have begun to know him myself. When I was a little fellow I used to fear him for he was then somewhat stern. But he was then very much a worried man with a dreary present and a bleak future and an array of little children depending on him."

As a boy on his father's farm, Cal had been seen as someone who might make his mark in the world. "In many respects," Jack recalled, "he was a precocious young lad, for when I got to Belleville I heard from the old-timers stories of Cal Dafoe's exploits."

Years later Jack would remember a moment when his usually taciturn father had revealed a previously unsuspected aspect of his character: "I was surprised too to one day find that my father had a good deal of family pride in him. What he said in effect was that while none of the Dafoes had ever amounted to much and were perhaps not a very clever family, they had all, so far as he knew, been honest and upright men whose word was as good as their bond. And I am somewhat proud of such a lineage, although my forefathers were a lot of rather rough and unlettered backwoodsmen. But they lived up to their lights and left a name that their sons were not ashamed of."

Even as a boy Jack was aware that his father had "a very tender heart in his big body" and he noted and remembered his father's kindly treatment of Mary, his wife. "She has by far the better judgment of the two and of late years particularly he has depended very largely on her opinions. They have lived very happily together." Looking back in young manhood, Jack paid tribute to his parents: "To one who knows as I know the limitations of their life, how few have been their opportunities for culture, how narrow has been the horizon which bounded their lives, they seem to have improved their chances. They are typical country folks, rough but warm hearted, stubborn in their likes and dislikes, upright and honest to an extreme."

"Cal Dafoe," his daughter Edith recalled in 1944, "could handle a plough or an axe, but he could not handle a pen. His wife did all his writing, except his signature on documents." Cal's wife, Mary Elcome, born at Wrotham, Kent, in 1840, thought highly of education, although she had spent little time in school herself. Mary, her daughter Edith remembered, had "desired above all things" to attend a real school, but education was hard to come by for the working poor in early Victorian England. She did manage to attend a dissenters' Sunday school for several years where she learned reading, writing and spelling, before getting a place at a "dame-school." She spent six happy weeks there. Then came the news that her mother had died. "She was the oldest girl and must be mother now. She was just fourteen." In 1857 her father, John Elcome, gathered up his five daughters and a son, Ted, and sailed to a new life in Canada, leaving behind several grown children from an earlier marriage. After a six-week voyage, the Elcome family settled at Zion's Hill, near Belleville, not far from Samuel Dafoe's farm.

In a letter written to an English granddaughter in 1871, Elcome set out his reasons for leaving his old home: "I often think I should like to take a peep at you all over there in Old England, for England with all her faults I love her still, but not well enough for to wish myself back again. No. No. I had enough of her bondage while living there ... You know as well as I can tell you that a labouring man in England can never become anything but a labouring man whilst here he can in a few years become a land owner and a freeholder and not only himself but his sons after him and their sons for several generations; and the daughters will be sure to marry men that have land of their own, while in England a man may work hard all his life till he is old and past work. And what then? Why he may go into the unions [workhouse] and be treated nearly as bad as a criminal who has broken the laws of his country. And if his dear old wife is still alive they will be separated. That's the biggest blot upon the laws of dear old England."

Visiting Belleville as a boy, Jack Dafoe saw the cottage where his mother had lived with her father, brother and sisters before her marriage: "A queer old fashioned English cottage standing back from the main highway. It was pretty well beaten and blackened by the storms of 30 or 40 years, but I can fancy that it was a very pretty place when my Grandfather lived there, for he was from Kent, England, and was therefore a lover of beautiful gardens."

Uneasy with his own father, the young boy enjoyed a close relationship with his grandfather Elcome, who died when Jack was seven. As a young man, Jack recalled happy times at his grandfather's fireside, with stories and music. "Poor old Grandfather!" he wrote in a letter, "how well I can remember him although he has been dead many long years. A queer old Englishman fond of his jokes and his grog, usually as merry as a lark, but with occasional lapses into fits of cantankerousness when the only one who had any control over him was my mother whom he used to call 'Molly.' In his young days he was one of the radical leaders of the Kentish yeomen of the great agrarian struggles 40 years or so ago against the land holders. I think he was imprisoned once or twice for heterodox remarks about the English aristocracy... the squires were highly pleased when he gave up the fight and moved to Canada. He was a violinist of more than average ability, but I regret to say that that characteristic I did not inherit, although when he died he left me his fiddle."

There was a school of sorts in the settlement where rudimentary lessons were given by volunteer local teachers, including, on occasion, Grandfather Elcome. It was the usual backwoods schoolhouse, with a pot-bellied stove and rough benches. Jack's sister Edith later recalled his eagerness to attend: "As soon as he was old enough to go to school nothing could keep him home—not weather, not lack of clothes. One day he faced the problem of no lunch. The supply of homemade bread had run short. He would have gone without a lunch, but compromised on some cold hotcakes left over from breakfast."

In 1873, about the time that John Elcome died, Jack's parents made the decision to send him "out front"—that is, out of the "backwoods" and "out front" to the settled area in which the family had originated—so that Mary's promising son could go to a proper school in a proper town. Jack would have the education Mary had once dreamed of for herself. Cal was probably easily talked into giving his approval. After all, young Jack wasn't much use on the farm anyway. Without making any formal arrangements, the parents assumed that the boy would stay with the Dafoe grandparents he had never met, Samuel and Eve, 100 miles away at their farm at Zion's Hill near Belleville. The seven-year-old made the journey on the stage coach under the supervision of an adult passenger. It was his first trip away from home and there was a sad surprise awaiting him at Zion's Hill. Both his grandparents were dead.

PUPIL TO TEACHER

The photograph itself has vanished, but, looking back, we can easily imagine the seven-year-old Jack Dafoe, like "Little Father Time," the travelling boy in Thomas Hardy's novel *Jude the Obscure*, arriving unexpectedly among his relatives at Zion's Hill, with his small bundle of possessions, an anxious expression on his face and a name tag pinned to his coat. "The earliest photo I ever had taken was a tin-type which mother keeps as one of her treasures," he wrote in a letter to his future wife in 1889. "When I was the mature age of seven I left home and went 100 miles by stage to friends whom I had never seen before to go to school. That was another specimen of infantile gall. One of my aunts took me into Belleville and had a tin-type taken of me which she sent home. I look like an impertinent young shaver and I guess that is what I was, for during the months I was away from home I was perpetually in scrapes with my aunts and uncles, with my school teacher, with the neighbours. I was regarded as incorrigible and I find that the echoes of my achievements still linger in that neighbourhood. I visit it occasionally and the people have gradually got used to seeing me as a respectable looking and apparently steady-going young man, but at first they were very much surprised for they had evidently predicted a worse fate for me." Among his later recollections of school days in Belleville was the memory of frequently being "kicked and cuffed" by his teachers.

There was also, undoubtedly, the disappointment of finding that the grandparents he had expected to meet for the first time and live with had died. He had just lost Grandfather Elcome and now these two unknown grandparents were gone too. Perhaps they had both died suddenly after falling prey to one of the sinister maladies that often struck unexpectedly in those days. From a twenty-first century perspective it seems odd that news of this family bereavement had not travelled the one hundred miles from Belleville to Combermere. There had been little communication between Cal and his parents. It may be that there had been bad feeling over Cal's decision to strike out on his own. It seems they were not letter-writing people. There were no telephones, no telegraph. News travelled slowly along the muddy road to the backwoods.

Jack's months at Zion's Hill may have been difficult, but the experience of meeting crowds of aunts, uncles and cousins made a strong impression on him. For the rest of his life he would set great store by family connections, however remote. "Every time I go to Zion's Hill," he wrote in 1889, "I have to visit cousins even to the third and fourth remove, aunts and grandaunts and really I never have anything to say. It is not so bad at Uncle George Simpson's for there are four—no five—girls there and we always succeeded in making things lively in the homestead." Teasing and horseplay invariably broke out when young Jack found himself surrounded by his Belleville cousins. At the time of his marriage in 1890 his cousin Nina Simpson remembered him as "a long-legged, lantern-jawed, spindle-shanked, red-headed curiosity," Jack responding: "This graphic summing up of my physical characteristics is no doubt in revenge for numerous vivid portraits by me of her rustic admirers." In 1873 young Jack was just the extra cousin, another mouth to feed, the bad boy from the backwoods, although his teacher had to admit that he was a promising pupil, skittish, a bit of a brat, but always at the head of his class.

As Jack began to get on his relatives' nerves, winter set in. There was no going back before spring or until somebody turned up and indicated a willingness to accompany a lively seven-year-old on the journey into the woods. In fact, he was to remain "out front" for 15 months before an opportunity finally came to put him on the stage for the trip home.

Then it was back to the local school, daily chores on the farm and the long agony of successive dreary Sundays. There were, however, compensations. He could escape into the woods. Looking back years later he recalled those backwoods days when he was free to ramble for miles, thinking the long thoughts of childhood and dreaming of the years to come. "I have a disposition tending toward melancholy," he would write when he was a few years older, "although I have always struggled against it. I am afraid I have not followed the injunction of the Greek sage: I do not know myself. Sometimes I despise obstacles and feel that I could wrestle with all the hydra-headed evils of the world: and again I am so weak, so fearful of the future, so doubtful of my strength that I am in despair." Like many lonely children he memorized poems and began to think of the possibility of being a poet himself. He found comfort in reading and in the beauty of the hills, lakes and woods around him. Looking back in the autumn of 1889 he found that in spite of the "cloudless days and calm nights" of his new Manitoba home, he wished sometimes that he was "once more in the Ontario backwoods so that I might see the mountains breaking into all the varying tints of crimson and gold at the touch of frost. I always loved trees: the sound of the wind soughing through the fir branches used, when I was a child, to have an uncanny sort of attraction for me."

He was reading poetry by now and he began to write some verse of his own. Edith later recalled her father's amused exasperation with his daydreaming son: "He always had his mind on his books, never on his work. Why we couldn't even send him to pick berries but he would lose his berries and the dish he picked them in and come home with a long string of verses about the Wars of the Roses or some such tom-foolery."

The poem about the Wars of the Roses, Edith recorded, was published in the local paper and later in the *Arnprior Chronicle* "and copied in many other publications." Jack would keep a faded clipping of the printed version of his poem, along with other early writings, for the rest of his life. The poem, called "A Bouquet of Flowers," was prefaced by a note from the local editor: "The following lines were read at a recent school entertainment in the village, by the lad who composed them, who is only 12 years of age. Perhaps their reproduction here may stimulate his schoolfellows to try to do even better."

The poem begins in flowery fashion: "I wandered through the forest, / I wandered by the well, / I wandered through the upland, / and by the flowery dell, / I plucked some pretty flowers — / The ones that I love best — / I bound them in a bouquet, / and pinned them to my breast." These, of course, are no ordinary flowers: "And, waving in the centre, / Is the Red, the Royal Rose: / I'll sing of it in poetry, / 'Twas never meant for prose..." Then, suddenly, we are plunged into history: "Many a year ago there met, /In battle's fierce array, / And the poor Red Rose was trampled on, / In many a fearful fray, / But finally she triumphed, / When, on fatal Bosworth's field, / Bold Richmond cleft the murderer's skull, / And forced the White to yield." The poem goes on for several more stanzas in similar vein, giving a hint of the sort of potted British history served up to Canadian schoolchildren in that era as well as marking the beginning of Jack's lifelong love of the old ballads of his mother's native land. Young Jack was blissfully unaware that "Bold Richmond" had nervously watched the battle from a safe distance.

Being published at 12 must have tempted the young poet to believe that he might have a future in letters. He was reading everything he could get his hands on, from history and adventure stories to the work of such poets as Tennyson and Longfellow. Cal must have looked on and wondered how much help he was going to be on the farm. Mary would later remind him that if Jack had been useful on the farm he would never have had the chance to go away to school, never have had the chance to make something of himself in the outside world. In 1879 Jack's father looked at him and saw a lazy dreamer. Aware that his stern father did not approve, Jack nevertheless went on reading and writing poetry.

A source of comfort during those years of early schooling at Combermere were the occasional visits of Uncle Edwin Elcome— Uncle Ted, his mother's brother—who, during that time, was beginning to prosper in the timber business. "I can well remember," Jack recalled in young manhood, "the sensation that Uncle Ted's arrival used to make at our household. He was always all summer taking a raft of timber to Quebec, but in the fall he was sure to come back with a valise full of toys and trinkets purchased in the far away world whose stir never penetrated to our house in the almost impenetrable pine forests and of whose splendours we children used to speculate in our wondering childish fashion. And so Uncle Ted was looked for with great enthusiasm." Uncle Ted would remain his favourite throughout his childhood and young manhood: "For him I have a very deep and sincere affection for he was kind to me when I was a little fellow and when I was not accustomed to being treated with much consideration." Uncle Ted's wife, Aunt Aggie, was another matter. "When I was a young lad," he later wrote, "I stayed with her for a couple of years and went to school and we fought every day of our lives. Possibly it was my fault, but she was the only woman I ever ran into that I could not get along with." Uncle Ted, however, "was one of the kindest hearted and most lovable men I ever met."

Uncle Ted came to the rescue again when Jack was 13. While the boy languished at the local school at Combermere, Ted Elcome and his wife had been establishing a home for their family in the town of Arnprior, which was then rising rapidly at the place where the Madawaska River meets the Ottawa. In 1879 he proposed that Jack come and live with his family and attend the Arnprior High School. At his wife's urging, Cal accompanied his delighted son to the railhead at Renfrew and put him aboard the Canada Central train for the short journey to Arnprior. Jack spent the summer cramming for the high school entrance exams and, in spite of the defects in his early education, he stood first in the entering class. He would later write: "I have always regretted keenly that I was a white headed boy at school. I was generally head of my class in the school room but on the playground I was useless. You may not believe it, but in those days I was shy. If I had developed myself then I would have been today a good athlete for I have the requisite strength." His painful shyness made him terrified of girls and the girls, noting his terror, teased him unmercifully. He was called "Shakespeare" because of his ability to write impromptu verse and was occasionally conscripted to write love poems for the bolder of his male classmates.

Throughout his teens he continued to produce poems, many of which survive in his neat, schoolboy hand in a lined 8 x 11 notebook, foxy with age. Like many schoolboy poets of that period and later, his work veers between morbid accounts of war, death and adolescent despair and sentimental descriptions of landscape, usually seen at sunset, inducing gloom. The old lined notebook shows poems on the deaths of Longfellow and Princess Alice, a nature poem on "The Waters of the Madawaska," an "in memoriam" on the assassination of President Garfield, a stirring ballad on the death of General Brock at Queenston in the War of 1812, clearly inspired by the famous Victorian print in which the general falls mortally wounded, crying, with his last breath, "Forward Brave York Volunteers!" The poem begins "And now the hardy volunteers rush on / And charge the foe beneath an awful fire, /And louder pealed the fierce exulting gun, / With awful voice it told its deep pent ire. / While Brock quite fearless of the leaden hail, / Pushed forward leading on his little band, / Their iron hearts at danger ne'er did quail." This strong note of Canadian patriotism is evident in many of the poems written after 1881 as he shed the colonial attitudes of his childhood, forsook "Mother England" and became aware of the history and beauty of his own country. A Canadian nationalist was born.

In common with many writers in the new Dominion he saw in nature a reflection of his own feelings and aspirations. In a brief lyric written in November 1882 he turned to healing nature as an antidote to the poisons of everyday life: ·

> Far from the never-ceasing strife,
> Far from the cares and woes of life,
> I tread the hillside wide and bare,
> To breathe the sweet, calm evening air.
> The gentle zephyrs hurrying by,
> The darkening dome of azure sky,
> The prattle of the mountain rill,
> The twilight hush so strangely still,
> Speak to my heart in tender tone,
> And dark misanthropy dethrone.

When he was slightly older and still writing poems, he cast a cool eye over his early verse, writing critical comments in the margin and drawing a rejecting line through those he considered unworthy juvenilia. He drew a line, but did not destroy them. They were too close to his heart to utterly reject and, like many of us, he kept his boyhood verses hidden away in a safe place for the rest of his life.

He would be grateful for his time at the Arnprior High School, but soon enough he would come to see the inadequacy of the secondary education offered to young people of his class in the

Canada of the 1870s. Leaving school, he was painfully aware of how much he did not know. The history of his own country was almost a closed book to him. He knew little of science. Although he was addicted to books, he was aware that his knowledge of literature, ancient and modern, was rudimentary at best. He knew no language but English. There was no place for him at any university. Education for him would be a lifetime process, through reading, observation and contact with other minds, for evermore the "sedulous ape." For the rest of his life he would be busy filling in the gaps and adding to what he had already learned. To a boy living in a town on the edge of the wilderness in a country in which cultural matters fell under the aegis of the Dominion Department of Agriculture the prospects must have been daunting. Perhaps this may have been the cause of the "breakdown" of some sort he appears to have suffered about this time.

"He had difficulties to meet that we at home knew nothing of," his sister Edith wrote in the 1940s. "He never complained about his shortage of books. Some he had, of course, but others he had to borrow and keep on borrowing days ahead of time so he could get his lessons ready before the owner needed it for his own preparation. ... He had been growing fast and studying hard and his aunt's doctor advised that he stop school for a while—so he came home." Shortly after he arrived home in the early spring of 1881 he celebrated his fifteenth birthday.

One of his biographers puts it this way: "At the age of fifteen he could not quite face the insecurities of the outside world, and went home to the log cabin to sit for long periods on the sunny steps, watching the flies and dreaming." It is easy to imagine his father's reaction to this languid homecoming, but the "rest cure" would not be a long one. Farm work did not attract him, but another temptation soon presented itself. His sister Edith would recall what happened next: "We had just formed a new school district and built a school house a half mile from our home, but would not be having a teacher until after the holidays. So he gathered up the youngsters of the neighbourhood and for a month or so he practiced teaching on them and that is all the normal training he ever had. After holidays he really went teaching, not in our school but up at Bark Lake." In a letter of 1889, Jack recalled his first taste of teaching in the local school: "I was just thinking last night that it is just nine years ago that I made my start in life. I must have had a lot of gall, or nerve, or cheek, or something, or I would never have undertaken to teach a country school. I started at the home school and I remember that on the morning when I started for the school I turned around at the gate and called out to mother 'First start in life!' and she answered 'May you be successful!'" Teaching the neighbours' children was an easy introduction for the young hopeful. It would prove to be a stiffer proposition when he went away from home later in the summer as a permit teacher, first at the Egan Estate Settlement— later called Murchison—and then at the new school at Bark Lake in Jones township.

Responding to a letter from the Rev. A.J. Reynolds of Killaloe, Ontario, in 1929, Jack recalled those far off but well-remembered days: "You are right in your supposition that it was I who taught school in the Egan Estate Settlement—or Murchison as it is now called—in the year 1881. I organized the school and was its first teacher; it was a rather nervy proposition for a youngster in his fifteenth year. When I turned up in the settlement one of the ladies there made the entirely just remark to me that I ought to be going to school instead of trying to teach one. I more than once walked the sixteen mile stretch of road which ran through the wilderness from the Settlement to Bark Lake; and I followed the invariable custom of the road by tarrying at your father's place, which was the only house in the whole sixteen miles." His landlady at Egan Estate Settlement, Mrs. Dunn, was a great matchmaker. "She had me married off three or four times while I was there," he remembered, "although I was not then sixteen years of age." In 1882, still unmarried, he moved on to the school at Bark Lake.

The settlement of Bark Lake, also known at the time as "Bullies' Acre," was located at a bulge in the Madawaska River about fifteen miles from the family farm. The settlement there was a kind of provisioning depot for the lumber camps where food and material were assembled and support trades such as black-smiths and harness-makers were located. It was a tough, hard drinking town, complete with gambling rooms and, possibly, a whorehouse. Young Jack had the task of organizing the school in the vicinity of all this rough vitality.

The young teacher seems to have made a favourable impression on his young pupils in the backwoods settlements. Years later he was to remark that "I have always been pleased at the staunch friendships I have always been able to make with little folks. When I was a teacher I was a prime favourite with the little ones. It often amuses me and pleases me too to recall the enthusiasm with which 'The Master' was received when he made his visits to the various households in the settlement." Jack, in fact, made friendships during his teaching days that lasted a lifetime, but not in the saloons or gambling dens of Bark Lake. As he would write in a letter in 1890 "I can drink anything in the tea or coffee line, I hasten to add by way of limitation. In the case of other drinks not so harmless in their nature, I can't (or at any rate don't) drink anything. Mainly because I never began and never intend to begin." Perhaps he saw too much wild drinking among the lumberjacks at Bark Lake to be tempted himself. He continued as he began and remained teetotal all his life.

A few years later, while living another sort of life, he looked back wistfully to his days as a backwoods school master: "I am gregarious. I like to meet people, study them, rub shoulders against them, but I was born in the woods and mountains and sometimes I have an overwhelming desire to get away from the fever and rush of city life. When I taught school I used to roam for hours over the stretches of hills once crowned with groves of pine but then browned and seared and desolated by recurring forest fires— doing nothing in particular but watching idly the wild landscape that stretched around—miles and miles of forest, unbroken save by a mountain lake here or there or by farms hewn out by hardy pioneers." This love of country places, lakes and woods would remain with him all his life.

"While teaching," his sister Edith remembered, "he kept up with his studies, sharing the kitchen table and the tallow candles with the other home workers of the family. And if the candle was suddenly and unceremoniously snatched away and they were left in darkness, he could rest his eyes and run his fingers through his hair until it was returned. The lady of the house no doubt needed it. She had many things to do and they could not all be done in daylight."

Young Jack had been called to Bark Lake to replace the former teacher who had reportedly died of drink, leaving behind a box of books and papers. Included in the legacy was a copy of Sir Archibald Alison's *History of Europe* and a volume of the collected orations of the British Liberal free traders John Bright and Richard Cobden. The views of Sir Archibald, an arch-Tory of the Lady Bracknell variety, appear to have had little, if any, effect other than possible amusement and hilarity, on the young teacher. The liberal and reform gospel of Cobden and Bright, however, hit him like a bombshell. Raised a Tory in an Orange household, the fifteen-year-old now began a pilgrimage that he would continue throughout his life. The final break with Toryism would come later, but the process of change had begun.

"When he came home at Christmas 1882," Edith recalled, "he was a man in size, if not in years. He looked like a big ruffian to us. He had bought himself clothes from the shantyman's store and a gorgeous tam-o'-shanter to top his bright red hair."

His teaching days were coming to an end. News of this under-age teacher in the backwoods had reached higher authority. His permit was to be lifted. He went back to Arnprior High School wondering what would become of him now. Looking back in 1890, he was amazed at how his life had unfolded. "When I look back ten years," he wrote, "and think of how much I have achieved that I did not even then dream of accomplishing I am conscious that I have been singularly fortunate. It seems a long time, too. Ten years ago I was just winding up my school days at Arnprior High School. I went back to the high school in 1883, but I only stayed a couple of months. I didn't like my teachers. Their names were Prof. Dawson and H.L. Slack and they were beauties. They used to come down to the school rooms reeling under the influence of liquor and when they got there they used to quarrel before the scholars. Dawson used to fresco the walls of the schoolroom with tobacco juice. I got so disgusted that I left school and went into newspaper work. So I suppose I should thank them for having disgusted me, otherwise my whole life might have been changed. I might still be a country teacher labouring away for a miniscule pit-tance. It is curious what tremendous results hinge on little things."

In February 1883 he opened a copy of the *Montreal Weekly Star* and read that there was an opening on the *Star* for "a young man of high ambitions." It was later suggested that Jack had long been dreaming of a career in journalism. Possibly it had crossed his mind, but it is more likely that the *Star*'s ad represented for him a possible escape from a life of backwoods school teaching and a stepping stone to a career as a man of letters. He would not be the first—or the last—young man to see a newspaper job as a stepping stone to literary glory. He picked up his pen and applied at once. As he was to observe later, "I have never for an instant regretted it. I doubt whether I would be worth my salt in any other business. I was born to be a scribbler and a scribbler I'll be all my life."

THE CUB EDITOR

Jack Dafoe's letter of application to the *Montreal Daily* and *Weekly Star*, written on 28 February 1883, has not survived, but the astonishing reply, handwritten by the *Star*'s managing editor F.G. O'Connor on 5 March of that year, has been carefully preserved as a family heirloom for more than a century. Addressed to "John Dafoe, Esq., Arnprior, Ont.," its arrival must have provoked a moment of extreme solemnity in the mind of the ambitious seventeen-year-old.

"My Dear Sir," it began, "Your favour of 28th Feb is before me. In reply I have to say that I should be glad to hear further from you in regard to your desire to come to the *Star* to learn journalism. What is your age and what are your ideas as to salary at first? We are not in the custom of paying beginners more than about enough to pay for their board. Have you a photograph that you could send me to enable me to form an estimate of your character?"

Mr. O'Connor's request for a photograph to help him "form an estimate of your character" suggests that he was a disciple of the Swiss theologian and author Johann Kaspar Lavater (1741-1801), remembered by some as the moving force behind the eighteenth-century revival of the ancient science of physiognomy or, as some called it, "characterology." It was Lavater's belief that moral character and intellect could be judged by a close study of the subject's outward appearance. There is no evidence that the

young applicant actually took the time to send a photograph—
or if he had one. It is possible that Mr. O'Connor got his first
glimpse of the young hopeful when he walked into his office on
the morning of 10 March.

Jack, in fact, had jumped on the first available train. Looking
back sixty years later, he remembered O'Connor as "a prince of
a man, a man of wide sensibilities and ideas. There was not one
chance in ten thousand that the average hard-boiled editor would
do what the editor of the *Montreal Star* did..."

"The *Star*," he recalled in 1943, "was not then the great paper that it is now. It had very humble quarters. I walked up a high
stairway of a building on Craig Street into a room where a lot of
young men were working very vigorously, supervised by a city
editor who was one of the best in the business that I ever knew;
and from there I went into another room where there were four
desks, and editors were at work. In a front corner room I found
Mr. O'Connor. I told him who I was and he looked at me a little surprised; and he puzzled for a while. 'Yes,' he said, 'we will
give you a trial.'" In spite of his uncouth appearance, his ill-fitting
suit and his unruly shock of red hair, young Jack had somehow
passed the Lavater Test.

Mr. O'Connor took another look at the tall, ungainly youth,
his big boots and his tam-o'-shanter and said: "You do not know
the city very well. We will give you some inside work." Jack, who
had arrived at the Quebec Gate station for the first time the night
before and who had rushed to the *Star* office from the hotel first
thing in the morning, became a cub editor at five dollars a week
instead of a cub reporter. The rustic outfit that had so disconcerted
Mr. O'Connor was too good to waste however. In July 1883 Jack
would wear it again when he undertook his first outdoor assignment for the *Star*.

A lifetime later, at the testimonial dinner marking his sixty
years in journalism, he would recall that early newspapering

adventure: "When I look back at my youth I wonder where I got the gall I had then and where I lost it. They put me to work and shortly after they sent me on the job of trapping a clothing store. They were building up a case against this store which was situated on St. Joseph Street near Bonaventure Station. The modus operandi was that a nice, green-looking young fellow going into the city would be picked up and asked if he did not want some clothing. Then the sharks would take him in and sell a good suit and then substitute a very inferior one. The *Star* editors decided that while they had quite a bit of evidence, they wanted to have it absolutely clinched and it occurred to them that the green lad was the boy to try it out. They equipped me with an old fashioned green travelling bag; I did not have to put on old clothes because I had them already. I went down to the station on circus day and wandered down St. Joseph Street carrying the carpet bag, and looking around on the wonders of Montreal and I was picked up at once. I went in and was taken up on the next floor.

"Meanwhile there were detectives outside—they were watching proceedings. I explained that I was from the country and had some money, and that I was going to have a good time in town and I thought I would buy a suit of clothes. Soon there were signals going on all over the place, which I noticed. They sold me a very good suit at a very good price and they said, 'You will get it as you go down the stair.' I got it—at least I got a parcel—and when I got out I headed for the detective's office. When I got there the editor of the *Star* was there and the business man who had put the *Star* on to this business. In the parcel there was a suit worth, perhaps, $2.15. I was very proud at having carried out my orders. I was for hiking back to the office. 'Oh no,' they said, 'you have to go back and raise a row by saying that you have been swindled.' That was not so hot, but my well known gall was summoned to the rescue and back I went with a couple of detectives following me; I went in and—Well!—they were the most astonished people;

they had a reputation unsullied; nobody ever had questioned anything they had done; and here was I, an ignorant country bumpkin, coming in and challenging their integrity. I made my protest and marched out and went back to the detectives' office and delivered the suit to them. It was all very thrilling for a kid of seventeen, believe me." The thrill was increased by the fact that the detective in the case was the celebrated John Fahey, who, by the end of the decade, was languishing himself in Longue Pointe penitentiary, himself a convicted felon.

"Well, the next week they started to expose the store; on the second day the *Star* was sued for libel; and the third day my story appeared in all its glory. It blew up the libel suit; it blew up the store, and it blew the swindlers out of Montreal."

This story, told in old age, may, like certain memories of Agincourt, have been "remembered with advantages." One of Dafoe's biographers has reported his failure to locate the "suit swindle" story in the *Star*'s files for 1883. This, of course, does not mean that something of the sort did not happen. It may well be that the edition of the paper in which the story appeared— and newspapers in those days often remade the front page several times every day—was not the edition that was placed on file at the end of the day. Newspapers often placed "scoops" in the second or third edition of the paper in order to confuse the opposition. In the headlong rush of daily journalism at the end of the nineteenth century such omissions undoubtedly took place. Jack's account of the adventure, recalled after sixty years, probably describes what happened, more or less.

Whatever the story was, it was not sufficiently sensational to propel the country boy into the ranks of the *Star*'s cub reporters. "As I was still not trusted on the streets," Jack recalled, "they gave me inside work to do and I used to write stirring articles. My specialty was to point out to the people who wrote the books that I reviewed that they did not know anything about their subjects.

I was particularly severe on young poets. I wrote a little poetry myself in those days and it may have been jealousy."

In 1883 Jack may have regarded his work at the newspaper as a temporary measure, a stepping stone on the path to literary fame. He was still writing poetry in those first months away from school, as this untitled lyric, written in November of that momentous year, indicates:

> The night is calm; fair Luna's silver light
> Streams through the window to my study here.
> The stars are sparkling in their azure height,
> The mighty forest, standing bare and sere,
> In the cold autumn air is still; and not a breeze
> Stirs its bare boughs: all nature is at rest,
> The birds, the beasts, the tempests and the trees,
> All things are slumbering save my aching breast.
> They throb and thunder in their might and foam.
> Nothing can stop the freshet's sweeping tide
> Until its strength is gone; then to their home
> The foam, the thunder and the surge subside.

Behind the façade of sophistication, however, the greenhorn could still look around him and be impressed. In the vibrant city of Montreal and even in the *Star* newsroom there was much to dazzle a young newcomer from the hinterland. History was all around him: "One of the survivors of an earlier day, both of journalism and political life, was an occasional visitor to the editorial offices of the *Star* during my first years there. I noted that every few days an old gentleman, somewhat decrepit, would come into the office and paw over the exchanges. The habit was evidently well-established as his visits were taken as a matter of course. One day I heard the editorial writer address him as Sir Francis, whereupon I identified him as Sir Francis Hincks, editor forty years earlier of the *Montreal Pilot*, colleague of Baldwin and Lafontaine in the battle for responsible government, premier of Canada in the early fifties, a consenting party to the merger of Liberals and Conservatives in 1854 to form the Liberal-Conservative party, the Imperial governor of various colonies, finance minister in Sir John A. Macdonald's government shortly after Confederation. He was then living in almost entire retirement in a small house behind a high brick wall. In August 1885 he died in that house, a victim to the smallpox epidemic of that year."

Jack's enthusiasm for Montreal and the *Star* newspaper— not to mention his youth—cannot have escaped the notice of Hugh Graham, the proprietor and founding partner of the paper. Graham, with George T. Lanigan and Marshall Scott, had founded the newspaper as "The Evening Star" in 1869 when Graham himself was barely out of his teens. He would shortly gain full control of the publication. The *Star* had struggled in its early years as a one-cent daily with many English-language rivals, but was on the verge of its years of greatest success when Jack joined the staff in 1883. The *Star* with its associated papers, the *Family Herald* and the *Standard*, would become a major power in Canadian journalism and Graham would end his career as Lord Atholstan, but in 1883 the paper was still small enough that a promising boy from the backwoods could catch the eye of the proprietor. Jack and Graham would be friends until Graham's death in 1938 and at several points during Jack's career his old boss would be there to do him a good turn.

Gradually, reporting assignments came Jack's way. He was sent to cover breaking news stories around Montreal and he was assigned to the "hotel beat," interviewing and reporting on important visitors to the city. He began making friends as well. One of them was George Iles, then the manager of the Windsor Hotel and many years Jack's senior. Iles would be a mentor to him and a lifelong friend, later moving to New York and putting the younger man in touch with writers and newspaper men in that city. They would exchange books and information and visit back and forth for sixty years.

Another new friend was a McGill student, W. H. Turner, who recalled sixty years later that his "first meeting with Dafoe was not in the *Star* office, but in the diggings of a classmate, George Wright. It was in our Senior Year, 1883-4. Wright came of one of the most influential families in the Ottawa District. When Dafoe came to Montreal he and George Wright shared a suite of rooms in one of Montreal's best boarding houses. Wright was the elder by five or six years." How Jack came to know the nephew of the Hon. Alonzo Wright, a prominent MP, is not known. Perhaps George Iles or Hugh Graham, owner of the *Star*, introduced them. Jack had Wright relations back in Ontario and, although he would have been, at best, a poor relation, he may have had a letter of introduction in his pocket when he reached Montreal. W.H. Turner later worked on the *Star* and in the years that followed he and Jack would be colleagues in the Press Gallery at Ottawa and in the West, remaining friends for life.

Commenting on his Montreal friendships a few years later he would note, in reference to Turner, that "we are much the same—both rebels and radicals and in most points our views disagree but little, but I was always less aggressive and more inclined to at least pity the other fellows before jumping on them. I have not much granite in my nature. Perhaps my life would be more successful if I had. I liked Turner's aggressiveness and he liked the charitable turn of my nature."

Another lifelong friendship formed during those Montreal days was with Arthur H.U. Colquhoun, then beginning a newspaper career at the *Star* that would later take him to Ottawa where he became the second editor of the *Journal* newspaper and to Toronto, where he worked on the old Empire before becoming deputy minister of education for Ontario. Turner, Colquhoun and Dafoe appear to have been the "Three Musketeers" of the *Star* newsroom. "Colquhoun," Jack would recall a few years later, "after Turner, the warmest friend I have, was a great favourite with both of us." Like young journalists in every generation, the trio often sat up late at night arguing about politics, literature and life. Five years Jack's senior and a graduate of McGill, Colquhoun seems to have assumed the role of journalistic mentor to the newcomer. At the end of a letter written to Jack in May 1885 he puts down a teasing challenge: "I hope you will write soon as I want some material upon which to attack you, and your last letter is not beside me." Another comment in the same letter gives us a quick glimpse of the brash nineteen-year-old from the backwoods, as seen by his older friend: "I have now leisure to enjoy your letters but wish they were a little longer. One has to read enough of you to get into your vein and then you are agreeable in print, which you never are *in corpore*."

In spite of their profound political differences, Colquhoun and Dafoe would remain friends until Jack's death, the taunting letters going back and forth over the decades, as in this blast from Jack in 1925 regarding a new magazine published by a Colquhoun hero, Sir John Willison: "I was quite intrigued... by your discovery that after years of wandering in the wilderness of radicalism I had at last attained the Nirvana of Toryism in company with Sir John and yourself. After receiving this information from you I awaited with great eagerness the first number of *Willison's Monthly*, prepared to adopt it as my guide and instructor for the rest of my life. Great was my disappointment; I read it through and the only thing I found in it with which I was in wholehearted agreement was a quotation from the *Manitoba Free Press*. I am afraid that you and Sir John will have to give me up as a lost soul."

The brash young greenhorn from Combermere learned fast on the job and it was not long before he was given his first political assignment: "In January 1884 Mr. O'Connor came to me and said 'How would you like to go up and report the parliamentary session?' I can see now that it was one chance in a thousand that a thing like that could happen, but at the time I took it as a matter of course. It was a recognition of my something-or-other and I sailed up to Ottawa where I was the parliamentary correspondent for the *Star* for the next two years."

Looking back, it seems odd that the *Star* would send a green youth not yet 18 to cover the national parliament. The paper was undoubtedly having staff problems at the time and O'Connor, desperate, possibly had no choice but to take a chance on a newcomer who had already shown himself to be a fast learner. Perhaps his early reading of Jack's physiognomy had convinced him that here was a lad with a great future. Perhaps there was a financial problem. The *Star* at that time was barely holding its own against such rivals as the *Gazette* and the *Herald*, two long-established journals. Jack's little outpost in Ottawa would be inexpensive and there was the hope that he would grow in the job.

Jack made the most of his opportunity. Looking back at the end of his life, he remembered those Ottawa days with pleasure: "My task as a correspondent was to write a column of exposition and comment on the day in Parliament and get it into the late night mail to reach Montreal in the morning. I had a good deal of free time and I spent much of it in an alcove in the Parliamentary Library which was given over to English literature. It was haunted to much the same extent by the youngest Member of Parliament—a handsome and attractive man still in his twenties. He was Charles Tupper the younger. We had much conversation about politics, our careers and so forth. Diagonally across the Parliamentary Library was an alcove given up to French literature. It, too, had a rather steady visitor in the person of a tall Member, still on the youngish side of life. He was a kindly, companionable man and I soon struck up a friendship with him. He was generally regarded as one whose career had not fulfilled its earlier promise. The man whose career was thus supposed to be over was Wilfrid Laurier."

Laurier was then in his 43rd year. In his book *Laurier: A Study in Canadian Politics*, written in 1922, Jack would describe just how moribund the future prime minister's political career was in that far-off year of 1884: "His interest in politics was, apparently, of the slightest. He was deskmate to Edward Blake, who carried on a tremendous campaign that session against the government's CPR proposals. Laurier's political activities consisted chiefly of being an acting secretary of sorts to the Liberal leader. He kept his references in order; handed him Hansards and blue books in turn; summoned the pages to clear away the impedimenta and to keep the glass of water replenished—little services which it was clear he was glad to do for one who engaged his ardent affection and admiration. There were memories in the House of Laurier's eloquence; but memories only. During that session he was almost silent. The tall courtly figure was a familiar sight in the chamber and in the library—particularly in the library ... but the golden voice was silent."

Subsequent commentators have tended to dismiss Jack's early dispatches from Ottawa as the outpourings of a callow youth, but Mr. O'Connor may have known what he was doing when he threw his protégé in at the deep end. Political reporting and commentary would grow more refined and less rhetorical with the passing of time, but in nineteenth-century Canada the so-called "slashing" style of journalistic expression was highly valued. Canadian history was unfolding at a gallop in 1884, but up in the press gallery at the old House of Commons, personalities and politics engaged the attention of the "ink-stained wretches" of the fourth estate. And what personalities they were. Jack would recall them vividly nearly a lifetime later: "As I looked down from the Gallery what had only been names to me suddenly became living, visible men. There to the Speaker's right was Sir John A. Macdonald, his weather-beaten furrowed, shrewd old countenance reflecting a smiling satisfaction with the scene. He was flanked by his colleagues, three of them Fathers of Confederation—Tupper, Tilley, Langevin. Directly across the wide centre aisle from Sir John, with the table and mace between them, sat Edward Blake, leader of the Liberals, his desk piled high with ammunition in the guise of documents. Sharing his desk was a man, tall, slender, still youthful, with a gentle, scholarly face—Wilfrid Laurier. Beyond there was a broken, aged figure—Alexander Mackenzie, former Prime Minister, and beside him, with bristling moustache and visage stern, sat Sir Richard Cartwright, eager to get at 'em."

In a speech delivered at Kingston in 1941 at an event commemorating the fiftieth anniversary of the funeral of John A. Macdonald, Jack described his impressions upon seeing the old leader for the first time. "What impression did Sir John, then in his seventies, make upon a very young writer who watched the proceedings of Parliament during four critical sessions from his eyrie in the Press Gallery of the old Commons chamber? While it was not one that led him to enlist in the legions which followed Sir John so faithfully, it left no doubt in his mind of the old chieftain's greatness, his capacity for leadership and his unfailing confidence in his policies as necessary for the salvation of Canada. Sir John had behind him in the Commons a large majority of devoted followers; and this seemed to represent a strength in the country that was overwhelming and permanent. The fighting Sir John of the earlier years, in this confidence of his invincibility, had mellowed into an elder statesman whose speeches in Parliament were largely friendly talks to his adoring followers. But at the time of life here noted, he left the heavy fighting to others. As he was the first leader of the Commons that I had ever seen, there were no standards to which I could then compare him; but in the following decades he could be compared to the prime ministers who followed him. Only Laurier approached him in effectiveness."

Sir John's oratorical style, as Jack recalled in 1941, "was pretty much in the style of today. That was still the day of elaborate,

pompous oratory, but Sir John's method was casual and conver-
sational, especially when he turned his back on the Opposition
and chatted with the serried ranks of the Conservatives. His wide
experience in debate, the range of his knowledge, his firm grasp
on the philosophy which underlay his policies, and the witty al-
lusions and sometimes droll stories with which he reinforced his
argument, made these contributions to the business of the House
or to the course of debate bright spots in the welter of oratory.
His position was so secure that often he was content to reply to
quite serious attacks with some facetious remark that would set
the Conservative majority cheering and laughing."

The old chief, Jack told his 1941 audience, "had very definite
principles as to how power, once obtained, should be employed;
they were based upon what he regarded as the interests of the
State. But for the attaining or retaining of power, the means were
justified by the end! Hence some pages of his record that do not
make uplifting reading. But, fortunately, Shakespeare's saying can
be reversed. The evil that men do is often interred with their bones;
the good lives on. In this, of course, Sir John was not unique. As
a politician he was the product of his times."

Jack never forgot that session of the fifth Canadian Parliament.
In a radio talk in 1937 and in what was to be his valedictory address to his fellow journalists in October 1943 he drew a vivid
picture of the view from the press gallery as it was revealed to
him in January 1884: "The opening of Parliament came and one
day I climbed the stairway of the old Parliament building, which
has since vanished from the face of the earth, burned during the
last war. That Commons chamber, which for over fifty years was
the chief arena for Canadian political discussion, was a gloomy
and stuffy place; from the galleries it had the appearance of a
deep pit, at the bottom of which the members swarmed. It was
enclosed by walls that rose sheer and unbroken, save for narrow
entrances, for perhaps twenty feet. From the top of these walls

the public galleries sloped upward and back to the outer walls. Gothic windows in these walls and skylights let in an uncertain measure of light and when this failed recourse was had to a huge circle of flaring gaslights up in the ceiling. After a long night's sitting, in hot weather especially, the atmosphere was hardly endurable. The debate on the Address from the Throne proceeded. I went up the stairway perhaps not much interested in politics, and I came down a fighting Grit and the man who converted me was a gentleman by the name of Edward Blake, so I got my doctrine at headquarters. I had heard preachers and revivalists who came around at intervals, but the idea that one could do with the English language what Edward Blake did that night swept me off my feet. Sir John made a reply to Blake—a very neat reply. He did not have to argue—he had sixty of a majority. It was not necessary for him to make an argument. He turned about and talked to his supporters, who wildly cheered him. Up in the Press Gallery the youngster decided to put his money on the other side."

This may sound like a "Road to Damascus" conversion, but it is clear from his letters of this period and after that Jack had been slowly drifting away from his family's old-fashioned Orange Toryism ever since, as a boy, he had first felt uncomfortable about joining his father and his Lodge brothers on their annual noisy march on 12 July down the road from Combermere to Maynooth to annoy and provoke the Irish Catholics. His recent reading of the speeches of Bright and Cobden had also put a puff of wind in the sails that were taking him away from the political faith of his fathers.

His conversion, which he announced in a letter to the family, did not go down well at home. The Dafoes of Combermere—in fact the voters of the Combermere area, almost to a man—were loyal supporters of the Hon. Mackenzie Bowell, Grand Master of the Orange Lodge, MP for North Hastings, Tory cabinet minister and future Prime Minister of Canada. The Dafoes read the

Belleville Intelligencer, Mr. Bowell's newspaper, and regarded it as almost equal to the voice of God. Jack could not have shocked them more if he had announced that he had joined the Jesuits. Father Cal took the news hard and, according to the later testimony of his daughter Edith, spent a wrathful hour pacing up and down the cabin denouncing his wayward son, with references to the "serpent's tooth" and the possible vengeance of the Almighty. Then he went to bed and slept soundly, his rant over and his volcanic anger vented. Sister Edith's anger could not be so easily turned off. She sat down by the candle and wrote her brother a stern letter of rebuke, quoting heavily from her father's recent diatribe and finally denouncing Jack as a "turn-coat." The letter was mailed and as the days passed Edith began to think that she had, perhaps, gone a bit too far in her jeremiad. A reply duly arrived. "By that time," she records, "I was heartily ashamed of what I had said." Expecting a rocket, she opened the letter and read the following mild reply: "Edith, if some day you discovered that, in the half-light of morning and because of your own unawakened state of mind, you had put your dress on wrong-side out, what would you do about it? I believe you would turn it right-side-out. Well, that is just what I did to my coat."

He was also beginning to think about where he stood in the world. His father's generation had looked to the old world for direction, but Jack, sitting in the press gallery and conversing with his new friends in the quiet corners of the Parliamentary Library, saw a new identity coming into view. "Whenever anybody asks me whether I am English or Scotch," he would write, "I tell them I am neither. Four generations of Canadians lie in Canadian graveyards: that surely entitles me to call myself Canadian. I expect to be prouder of the name twenty years from now than I am today for then I hope to be able to say that I am a citizen of no mean country, not that I am a colonist. I am afraid that I am hopelessly radical." Worries about Canadian identity would haunt him all his life. Years later, in 1921, he would be forced to admit that his early hopes for Canadian nationalism were premature: "We have decided that our own Supreme Court was not good enough for the people of Canada, we have never had enough national spirit to provide ourselves with a distinctive flag; we have people in Canada objecting to standing up when O Canada is sung, we have trifled with the question of citizenship and nationality until the young Canadian is never sure whether he is a Canadian or a Hottentot because he had a Hottentot grandmother. We have put enthusiasm into every national day but our own."

Parliament rose early in 1884 and instead of returning to Montreal, Jack was given another chance to learn on the job: "My kind chief gave the boy another highly interesting assignment, sending me to Quebec to cover the Quebec Legislature; and I had six weeks in the ancient capital under conditions which enabled me to explore every nook and corner of that city and its neighbourhood. The Liberal opposition was limited to a mere handful of members, but it included one former premier of the province, Henri Joly de Lothiniere, two future premiers, Mercier and Marchand, and F.X. Lemieux, who was beginning a great career in politics and law, ending on the bench. With all these I established friendly relations, and in many ways I found my experience at Quebec in after life most valuable."

He spent a lot of time, as well, soaking up history and atmosphere, as well as indulging in a bit if mild flirtation. "It was in May and June 1884 and the old city was very beautiful. I was only a boy then with a boy's light heart, and I took keen enjoyment out of my experiences. I hadn't much to do, and so I used to wander away with a book to the grassy slopes of Cape Diamond and sit on the mounds thrown up by Champlain which have survived so many changes. I used to read and dream and build castles in the air. If I remember rightly I got into quite a flirtation with a petty little Irish girl who was a clerk in the bookstore where I bought my books. She was quite a coquettish young person. We got on very good terms, but she did not know who I was until one of the members of the legislature and I went in after some papers one day and he gave me away as the correspondent of the *Star*. 'Oh,' she said, 'so you're Mr. Dafoe.' Evidently my fame had reached her ears, and I suddenly felt filled with my own importance. But the flirtation was a very mild one and I wasn't particularly susceptible just then and so this vision of pure Irish beauty passed on out of my life and did not even leave me the memory of her name."

There is evidence that another and much more important flowering of youthful passion had also taken place back at the office in Montreal. There had been two women working in the *Star* office in 1883 and Jack appears to have fallen for one of them. Her name was Annette Parmelee.

ALICE AND ANNETTE

On Jack's first day as an "inside worker" at the *Star*, Mr. O'Connor had taken him into the small office next to his and introduced him to Annette Parmelee, a young woman who would have a profound influence upon his life.

He was to be, among other things, her assistant. Miss Parmelee was the *Star*'s "woman of all work," in charge of book reviews, contests, letters-to-the-editor, reader advice, clipping, library duties and all the other tasks that the "outdoor journalists" and the senior editors were too busy or too proud to do. Born at Montpelier, Vermont, in 1858, Miss Parmelee was the lively and up-to-date daughter of William Grannis Parmelee of Waterloo, Quebec, and his wife, Marcella A. Whitney of Montpelier, an American. William Parmelee was born in Waterloo, Quebec, in 1833, the son of Dr. Rotus Parmelee and his wife, the former Sara M. Grannis. The Parmelees appear to have been one of those nineteenth-century families that drifted back and forth across the border between the Eastern Townships and the United States from generation to generation, although Dr. Rotus Parmelee eventually went farther afield, settling with some of his family at Forrest Grove, Oregon. The family of W.G. Parmelee had returned to Waterloo in 1861 and in 1876 Mr. Parmelee, who was experienced in banking, insurance and railways, entered the Canadian Civil Service at Ottawa as chief clerk and accountant in the Customs Department. He would later set up and head the Department of Trade and Commerce as Deputy Minister.

Well-educated and independent-minded, Annette Parmelee
was not content to remain at home with mother until she found
a husband. Newspaper work was not an obvious choice of career
for young middle class women in the 1880s and we do not know
how Annette talked her parents into allowing her to take a job
in Montreal, but there she was in November 1881 working as a
proofreader at the *Star* and hoping for something better. Perhaps
her father was acquainted with Hugh Graham, the proprietor of
the paper. Possibly a relative, Charles Henry Parmelee, a future
King's Printer, who was working as an editor in Montreal in the
early 1880s, found the post for her. She was happy to have it, but
by February 1882 she was impatiently awaiting promotion. In a
letter to her sister Alice, who was just about to celebrate her six-
teenth birthday, she commented on her progress: "I am not getting along very fast except in promises. Mr. O'Connor makes me
a new and more brilliant offer about once a week and throws in
lots of flattery of a delicate kind to boot—but I am still holding
copy... He said that he would give me nice work in the office—the
'Educational and Etiquette' departments (which were his last offer), book reviews and things of that sort." So far, however, she appeared to have reached the Victorian equivalent of the glass ceiling.

But there was a surprise in store for Miss Parmelee. Later in
the month she reported to Alice that Mr. O'Connor was coming
back from a trip to Boston "in time to install me in my new place.
I expect I shall be ill at ease for a little while for it will be an entirely new departure for Montreal for a lady to be in the editorial
room. However, with Mr. O'Connor to back me I am not afraid
but what I shall get on all right."

A month later she wrote to Alice: "I am an editor now. Mr.
O'Connor had nearly half of his room partitioned off for me and
I can assure you I feel grand, as Mr. O'Connor and I are the only
ones who have rooms alone. I wrote my first book review today—
have four more to write tomorrow for Saturday's *Star*. I will send

up a paper." Safely tucked up in her little office, screened from the rough male language of the newsroom, Annette got down to work. In March 1883 the big red-headed boy from the backwoods arrived to be her assistant. Jack appears to have fallen for her almost at first sight.

He had never met a woman like her. Well-educated, intelligent, good-looking, independent, ambitious, well-connected, Annette Parmelee must have seemed like a character out of a novel by George Eliot, Charlotte Bronte or Elizabeth Gaskell. She read his poems and liked some of them, marking them with her initials and comments. She gave him books to review. She discussed literature and life with him and encouraged him to write. She surprised him by being annoyed when he compared her to Dorothea Brooke in *Middlemarch*. They would be friends and exchange letters until her death in 1918.

In 1883 she appears to have taken pains to let him down gently. The age difference of eight years was undoubtedly a consideration, but it was also a sobering fact that she would be leaving the *Star* later in the year to be married to Allan Ingalls, a young lawyer. In letters written to Jack from Ottawa in late 1883 she refers to herself as "your sister (by adoption)," which may well mean that she had convinced him to be "just friends" or, at best, "like brother and sister." She also teases him about possible flirtations with a "Miss Frost" and urges him to assure Miss Frost that his letter from Ottawa is of a business nature, "so she must not be jealous." In a letter written early in December she makes the following observation: "So you and Miss Frost have lost no time in starting theological discussions—well, I only hope they will all end as amicably as ours did—yours and mine..." With her wedding drawing near, she comments: "It seems like four months since I left the *Star*, and my two years there are already almost a dream, so great is the effect of my surroundings upon me. If I am ever again so happy as I was there, it will necessarily be a different kind of happiness—and I wonder if it could be a better kind! (Never reveal that such a speculation has entered my mind!)."

As she prepared for her wedding in Ottawa, she kept up a connection with the *Star*. Jack sent her books to review, but she was in such a muddle that her brain would not work. "Such a time as I am having trying to get that review written. I never have a solitary idea when I am in Ottawa and I am interrupted every five minutes. Yesterday I went up to the Parliamentary Library, but did not succeed much better there—just got started when it was time to close and the messenger jangled his keys until I took the hint and came home. I have sent off the review and it is a dreadful affair—I am heartily ashamed of it; scarcely know what is in it. I am lonely without you all; it seems a month since I left Montreal. Write to me."

Annette's December 1883 letter to Jack—and the many letters that followed in the years ahead—was full of queries and comments, a sort of slow-motion long-distance conversation of the sort that a future generation of young friends would conduct more swiftly with the aid of the laptop and the Blackberry. What did he think of *The Week*? "I saw a copy last night, but did not have time to read it. Its 'makeup' is something after the style of the *Literary World*, I thought. I saw Edgar Fawcett's name down as a contributor of two articles, what are they like?" She agrees with Jack that F. Marion Crawford, the author of such sappy historical romances as *Don Orsino* and *The White Sister*, has "mighty little common sense" to write so much in so short a time. "Perhaps," she comments, "he foresees that his sun will soon set and wishes to make hay while the sun shines." She had seen and rather enjoyed a comic opera, *The Queen's Lace Handkerchief*, staged by the theatrical company that had earlier presented *Iolanthe* by Gilbert and Sullivan. But, oh my, what a waste of time most of it was! "Last evening I spent out—on invitation—and played cribbage most of the evening with Mr. Parlow, head teacher of the

Model School, an old friend of ours. I beat him. Why do people with ideas spend time over cards? I enjoyed myself much, but should have liked better to talk to Mr. Parlow, who is well-informed, shrewd and entertaining—but when one is in Rome! For my part I should like better to be somewhere else—in Montreal, for instance. I expect my brother Charles up Saturday, Mr. Ingalls Friday. What a dreadful thing a wedding is, be it never so humble! I shall be thankful when mine is over."

In the same letter she rejects his modest estimate of his own ability as a correspondent: "You are very much mistaken, Sir; epistolary writing is certainly your forte, and I don't believe I shall ever be generous enough to absolve you of your promise to write to me, though I shall try to be as merciful as my nature will allow. Shall I confess that I enjoyed your letter so much that I couldn't keep it all to myself, but gave it to my sister Alice to read? I will not do such a thing again if you say I mustn't, but Alice and I are one and she enjoyed reading it as much as I knew she would." Her letters, on the other hand, were for his eyes only: "I forbid you to show my letters to anyone; other people might misunderstand my frank remarks—I know you will not, for are you not my brother? I grant myself the privilege of saying what I choose to you—of making my letters to you a sort of safety valve, should I need such a thing."

Perhaps an idea was forming in her mind when she mentioned that she had let Alice read his letter. As her own wedding day drew near, Annette may have decided to try a bit of matchmaking herself. One short sentence was all it took to bait the hook: "You must know my little sister; you cannot help being friends." After all, Alice, born in 1867, was only a few months younger than Jack. They might all be friends together and who knew what might happen when the two youngsters grew a little older. You can almost read Annette's mind.

In fact, as she knew perfectly well, Jack had already met Alice. "It was about the middle of July—in short July 16th when you were in the *Star* office," he would later recall. "I remember the date because it was on the following day, the 17th, when I played detective for a whole day in the interests of the *Star*." Was he wearing his country bumpkin outfit when he was introduced to Alice in the *Star* office that day in July 1883? If he was wearing it in anticipation of his role in the exposure of the dishonest tailors, it may well explain, in part, the difficulties he was to face in his attempts over much of the rest of the decade to woo Annette's little sister. First impressions, after all, can be crucial.

Jack, for his part, had his own first impression on that July day in 1883 and it may have given him hope that he might, in a curious way, recover what he seemed to have lost. Years later he would write to the girl he called his "Little Yankee:" "I thought that you were a miniature edition of your sister and felt a premonition in my heart that you and I would meet again." He was willing to admit that he had a hopelessly romantic nature. "I was always a precocious youngster," he would admit, "and I had several twinges of the grand malady before I went to Montreal, but they were the twinkling of the morning stars before the sun rose. I was of the mature age of 17 when I met you and fell in love again—this time to stay. I may not be very bright, but I generally know what I want and I get it—or know the reason why."

In a letter to Alice written in November 1889, Jack would attempt to explain how his friendship with Annette came to animate his early feelings for her younger sister: "One thing impresses me more and more and that is the essential similarity between yours and Annette's natures. I mean in your mental characteristics more than in your physical. I see it cropping up continually. Annette and I have been regular correspondents for the past six years and the likeness shows strongly in your correspondence and extends even to the handwriting. I was discussing the matter with Annette one day and she said she believed you were very much like one another, only yours was the more rounded and evenly developed nature—and I think she expressed the difference well. In both I see your father's strong nature softened and feminized."

When he went up to Ottawa in January 1884 to cover Parliament for the *Star* he was under orders from Annette to look up her family at their home at 261 Maria Street. "You will like my people, I am convinced, if you will only become thoroughly acquainted with them, and they cannot help liking you. You have already met my sister Alice, my oldest sister, and did not find her at all formidable did you? Well she is the cleverest member of the family so you need have no fears of the rest. They are likely to be as afraid of you as you are of them."

"Find you formidable?" he would ask Alice. "Well I should say I did. Why for five years after that letter was written I was more scared of you than of any person in the world. I used even to think of you with bated breath." That first visit to Maria Street made a strong impression: "Do I remember the first day I ever rang the doorbell of the Parmelee Mansion? Well I should say so. You came out of the sitting room to the hall to meet me. There were a lot of other people there. I don't remember who they were, but I remember how you looked. You were then just sweet seventeen and my heart jumped when I saw you coming. It was then that I began to recognize that it was all up with me."

Later he would confess to Alice that he felt a bit timid on those first visits. "I am conscious of still being deficient in many of the customs which hold in society. Seeing that my life has been spent mainly at my desk or alone in my chamber it is not to be wondered at—and I have no doubt that you will have considerable coaching to do. I am glad that you did not even long ago think me altogether uncouth. I sometimes thought that I must so impress you and that you were all too kindly and charitable to notice it. One of the reasons why I always liked visiting your place was that I was always put at my ease so completely."

Alice Parmelee, a mild and peaceable woman all her days, would later shock and amaze her grandchildren with hair-raising tales of her famous American ancestor, the redoubtable Hannah Dustin, who, in 1697, was taken prisoner with her baby during an Indian raid on her home settlement in the Massachusetts colony. Later, on the trail to New France, Goodwife Dustin, mourning the death of her child at the hands of her captors, turned the tables on the war party by waiting until they had fallen into a whisky-induced sleep and then killing and scalping them, returning in triumph to New England with her trophies.

The Parmelees were a large and lively family. There were eight children in all, five still living at home when Jack first presented himself at the front door of 261 Maria Street in 1884. On most nights the house was full of visitors, playing cards, chatting, singing around the piano and, most startling to a young man of backwoods Methodist upbringing, dancing.

Mr. Parmelee loved cribbage and whist and Jack eventually became a regular participant, aware that his mother back home in Combermere would strongly disapprove. "I think," he would later write, "something that unconsciously aided me in giving me a dislike of the Methodist Church was that its influence over me did not fail until I had passed the period when I had plenty of opportunity to learn to dance and thereby I sacrificed a great deal of personal pleasure to a stupid and unreasoning prejudice. I used some times to regret that I could not dance when they began to dance after the card playing." Jack was the wallflower, watching in agony as other young men danced with Alice.

Perhaps this is why he seems to have been shy about attending the Parmelee gatherings during his first months in Ottawa. In a letter written in March 1884, Annette chided him for staying away: "I am glad that you visit my people, but I am sorry that you can't go oftener—that is, if you like to go. I had a letter from my sister Alice a while ago in which she speaks of you as going there occasionally on Saturdays."

So he persevered and as the weeks went by he gradually became a regular visitor, liked especially by Alice's and Annette's father who enjoyed their games of cribbage and their long conversations. Jack quickly became fond of Mr. Parmelee, who seemed to have many of the qualities he had missed in his own father. "I don't know any man to whom my heart ever went out quite so much as to him," he would later tell Alice, "although even five years ago when I went around to Maria Street ostensibly to play cribbage with him, he was not the attraction. Do you know I fancy your father knew I was in love with you long before you awoke to the fact." And so the evenings at Maria Street went slowly by, with Jack playing cribbage with Mr. Parmelee, gossiping about doings on Parliament Hill and, out of the corner of his eye, furtively watching Alice chatting and singing with her friends at the other end of the room, seemingly unaware of his presence.

He went on outings with the family and gradually became more or less at ease with Alice's two younger sisters, Elizabeth and Julia, and her two younger hockey-playing brothers, James and Wilfred. On one occasion they went as a group with Annette and her husband Allan Ingalls to the public gallery at the House of Commons to listen to a debate. Years later Jack recorded in a letter to Alice his frustration at being unable to walk beside her and his acute embarrassment at displaying his seeming ignorance of some of the curious tribal customs of the day. "When I was walking side by side with Annette down the broad stone stairway I quite unconsciously in speaking of you to her called you 'Alice' in place of 'Miss Parmelee' and was quite horrified immediately afterwards at my temerity. You were some steps behind and did not hear me. I walked home with Annette and Bessie while you came behind with Allan. I remember Bessie insisted on keeping Annette between me and her and when we crossed a street and

I changed off to the outside Bessie moved to the other side of Annette. Finally I asked Bessie if she was afraid I'd eat her if she walked beside me for a block, but she only tossed her head and marched on." Some of those curious Victorian tribal customs endured well into the following century. As late as 1950 Great Aunt Bess was overcome with indignation when some oaf referred to her younger sister Julia as "Miss Parmelee." Casting a withering look at the offender, Bess intoned "I am Miss Parmelee. She is Miss Julia Parmelee."

In the autumn of 1885 Jack went out to the Townships to attend the wedding of one of the Parmelee's elder sons, Charles. He had hoped that he would meet Alice at the wedding, but she was detained in Ottawa by illness and he sadly continued his journey down Lake Memphremagog to Newport, stopping off to visit the Ingalls at Granby on the way back. "Allan and I had a pretty high time of it, shooting and fishing and I remember Allan in one of his confidential moods waxing quite eloquent over the virtues of the Parmelees. He said some very complimentary things about you," he would one day report to Alice. "He hadn't the slightest suspicion that the young lad stretched full length on the grass listening to him could have taken up the stories of your good qualities and double discounted his brotherly eloquence. For I went home from the long Parliamentary session of 1885 as madly in love with you as it is possible for a young man of 19 to be—and that's the age that young people can take love very hard."

He would suffer and languish through the remainder of 1885 and into the following year. In the summer of 1886 he took his courage in both hands and asked her, by letter, to be his wife. The letter of proposal was enclosed, sealed, in a letter to her father. Jack, faithful to the conventions of the age, was seeking parental approval of his suit. The first hurdle was cleared easily. Mr. Parmelee handed the unopened letter of proposal to Alice. She replied to Jack, also by letter, on 24 August: "Dear Mr. Dafoe,

'Tis difficult to find words to express to you my surprise and sorrow. I cannot answer you as you wish. I can never entertain for you any stronger regard than that of friendship. Let me still be sincerely your friend, Alice Parmelee."

Her reasons for refusing him remain unknown. Perhaps she felt that she was too young to marry. Possibly she was bothered by the difference in their backgrounds and worried about the possibly uncouth backwoods relations at Combermere. It may be that she was aware that they would make an odd couple—he was six foot four, she was less than five feet. She was an Anglican, he a backsliding Methodist. Possibly, like many young Victorian women of her class, she was not yet ready to contemplate the more basic realities of married life. On the other hand, it may be that Alice, steeped in Victorian literature of the sort written by such authors as Anthony Trollope, George Eliot and Charles Dickens, subscribed to the notion that no young man should ever be accepted at the first proposal. The fact that the letter of proposal was postmarked "Winnipeg" undoubtedly played a part in her quick decision to decline. Still a teenager, she may have been understandably reluctant to leave her parents and the safety of her home for a new and possibly alarming life in what would have seemed to her to be "the back of beyond," the Wild West.

Years later, in April 1889, when she had finally changed her mind, Jack would look back to that first proposal with a shiver, recalling the day "when I wrote the famous letter which as you confessed to me first made you aware that you were no longer a little girl but a young woman and which I think took a good deal of the boyishness out of me. I hesitated and trembled a good deal before writing it and it is one of the actions of my life that I am really proud of, that I had the courage to write that letter. As I said above, it made a man of me. I was badly cut up over your reply which I now have within reach of my arm, but the young man of 20 is sanguine and I never for one moment thought of taking that as final."

He had been turned down, but, as he told her in 1889, "Had I not written that you might indeed have forgotten me and you would have met me almost as a stranger. And my calculations were in a measure right for you have admitted that you used sometimes to re-read my first faint effort in the love-making line."

Jack was cut up, but not downhearted. He would try again, but he would have to travel many miles and have many adventures and disappointments before he gained his heart's desire.

THE RISE AND FALL OF AN EDITOR

While Jack carried on his shy, unsuccessful courtship in the front parlour at 261 Maria Street, his journalistic career was nevertheless moving along briskly. Looking back in old age he saw those far-off days clearly. "The year 1885 was politically big with fate," he remembered in the last year of his life. "At the opening of the session of Parliament, which I again attended, the government of Sir John A. Macdonald seemed as impregnable as ever, but before the year was out it was faced with a question which had dynamite in it no matter how it was dealt with. This was the North West Rebellion and the problem of Louis Riel's fate. In the late winter we began to hear rumours of trouble on the banks of the Saskatchewan. Assured by the Superintendant of Indian Affairs that this was idle and mischievous gossip, I walked directly over to the Press Gallery and got there just in time to hear Sir Hector Langevin announce the outbreak of the rebellion and the slaughter of the police and settlers by the insurgents."

It was a golden moment for a young, ambitious journalist to find himself in Ottawa with a seat in the Press Gallery, although there must have been moments when Jack envied the reporters who had been sent out west to cover the action on the Saskatchewan. Events that would shape the course of Canadian politics for decades to come were unfolding day by day. "Eventually," he would recall a lifetime later, "the rebellion was put down and Riel was captured. He was found guilty of treason at Regina by a jury, with a recommendation to mercy arising from the jury's doubts as to his sanity. What was to be his fate? Should he be hanged or should his sentence be commuted? There were two roads for the government to follow, and there was trouble along either road. The decision of the government was a closely kept secret and I was rather staggered when I was assigned to find out whether Riel was to hang or not. I went up to Ottawa and skirmished around officials. I found a hunch everywhere that he was going to be hanged. One prominent civil servant, well on the inside, Henry J. Morgan, said to me 'I don't know anything about it, but you can bet your last money that Riel is going to be hanged.' So, bold as brass, I wired the *Star* that the hanging would proceed according to plan."

The execution of Louis Riel was to cast a long shadow over Canadian politics, extending deep into the next century. One immediate effect was the unexpected resurrection of the political career of Jack's Parliamentary Library acquaintance Wilfrid Laurier. As the future prime minister's star rose again, the young journalist looked on in a glow of admiration that remained undimmed over half a century later: "Addressing a vast meeting on the Champ de Mars in Montreal he made the famous remark that if he had been living on the banks of the Saskatchewan in the spring of 1885 he would himself have shouldered his musket. He then invaded Ontario and addressed a series of meetings. His charm of manner, far surpassing that of any public man I have ever known, his complete fearlessness in facing hostile audiences, and the power of his eloquence, gave him a position in the Liberal party and in public regard that made his selection as leader inevitable when Blake, following the defeat of 1887, threw up his hands." In the years ahead Jack would frequently disagree with Laurier, he would come to see that the Liberal leader "had affinities with Macchiavelli as well as with Sir Galahad," but happy memories of that glorious re-awakening of 1885 he would carry to the end of his life.

"The next session of Parliament," Jack would recall, "saw, in April 1886, the debate on the execution of Riel. It took place on a resolution moved by a French Conservative Member condemning the government for not commuting the sentence. It was notable for three speeches—that by Laurier, who, in the opinion of many, reached the high-water mark of his eloquence; by Blake, who would join the condemnation of the government; and by the new Minister of Justice, John Thompson, who on this occasion first revealed his quality to the House. The question became an open one, and in the resulting division about half the French Conservatives voted against the government and half the Ontario Liberals voted with the government—a remarkable performance bearing in mind the strong party feeling in those days."

As the smoke of battle dispersed over Batoche and old political alliances broke apart in Ottawa, young Jack, possibly dazzled by the excitement of it all, made a decision that could have ended his newspaper career. "In the late months of 1885," he remembered in old age, "the owner of a large printing establishment in Ottawa decided to issue a daily paper. He offered me the editorship and with a recklessness which I still admire but cannot now understand, I took on the job." He was 19.

The offer, hand-written on notepaper headed "The Senate," reached him at the *Star* office in Montreal in the second week of October 1885. It read: "Dear Dafoe, Mr. A.S. Woodburn is about to start an evening paper here, and wants an editor who is not the slave of either party. We do not know whether you are free for such an engagement: if you are, he would like to hear from you at once. His address is 36 Elgin Street. If you could not undertake the work, do you know of anyone who could fill the bill? Please reply promptly as he wishes to issue the first number on Nov. 1st." The letter was signed Geo. C. Holland.

The would-be publisher of the new paper, A.S. Woodburn, was, presumably, unknown to Jack, but he would have known

George C. Holland, an experienced journalist who, with his brother Andrew, had been contractor for reporting and publishing the Senate debates since 1875. It can be imagined that young Jack took about two seconds to decide that he was ready and able to become the first editor of the *Ottawa Journal*. It was a bold and foolhardy decision for a youth of limited journalistic experience, but, like the child thrown off the dock at the deep end, he swiftly found himself learning to swim at least well enough to keep his head above water.

As editor, he struggled to follow the non-partisan mandate laid down by his proprietor, enthusiastically slapping the Liberals before turning to swat the Conservatives. He supported Home Rule for Ireland and stood up for Canadian fishing rights on the East Coast. He poured cold water on proposals for a railway and seaport route for Hudson Bay, a cause he would later vigorously champion. He took a stand against the dangers of socialism and urged Quebeckers to learn English and try to assimilate. The paper took a dim view of a commercial union with the United States. It firmly rejected the notion of a "Super-Parliament" to govern the British Empire from "Headquarters" in London, a proposal that would attract Jack's hot opposition for decades to come, whether proposed by Lord Curzon or Rudyard Kipling. For the *Journal*, each day brought its own big issue, its own surprise to the bemused readers of the newspaper. Jack was at some pains to explain the non-partisan nature of the paper, invoking the figure of the Mugwump as a symbol of the *Journal*'s mission to be critical of all sides in the political struggle. "Great is the Mugwump and his mission is to teach the divine right of bolting. May his shadow never grow less" he ranted in one early editorial effusion.

In a letter to Alice Parmelee written in June 1889 Jack summed up his first experience as an editor: "To this day I have never got over the six months I put in at the *Journal*. Of course we were starting the paper and at the outset my staff was a poor one. I was trying to make bricks without straw. It so angered me to see the way some of them did the work that I went in for doing everything I could myself. I used to go down to the office at 6:30 in the morning and it was rarely that I locked up before 11 at night. Then I worried a lot for Mr. Woodburn had no more idea of running the counting room end of the paper than I had of Sanskrit. Still my clouds had a silver lining for could I not usually see you once a week? I don't believe I missed many Saturday nights during those six months."

The *Journal* was one of many newspapers launched in the 1880s that claimed to be superior to party politics and interested chiefly in news. Such papers, which came to be known as "the However and Nevertheless Sheets," had to walk carefully in order to avoid giving too much offence to their politically committed readers. Jack would later recall that "In the Montreal which I first knew there were, for a period of some years, six daily newspapers in English and at least five in French. As purveyors of news their services were rudimentary. The telegraph companies of that day carried a news service of sorts and most newspapers were content with this supplemented by an occasional special from Ottawa and the larger cities. When I launched the *Ottawa Journal* I solved the problem of outside news with great ease. I went down to the Great North-Western Telegraph offices and contracted for a service for which I paid the staggering sum of $15 a week." Items from out-of- town papers were also perused, clipped and made use of, as were gleanings from the overseas press. Short fiction, book reviews and contests also helped to fill space on slow days.

The historian Ramsay Cook, writing of Jack's brief stint at the *Journal*, took a tolerant view of the inexperienced, often ill-informed, somewhat bumptious, young editor's efforts to establish the new paper: "Undoubtedly," he wrote, "the paper was directed by a bright, studious, young mind anxious to promote, as one editorial was headed, 'The Science and Study of Politics.' The editor was full of self-confidence and not inclined to serve any master. Obviously he was writing about himself when he remarked on one occasion that 'The most striking characteristic of young men is a repugnance to being led by the nose.' Indeed, the quality of the whole paper, during Dafoe's term of office, was that of a very good undergraduate production. And why not? But for his lack of means Dafoe would probably have been at a university during these years instead of attempting to run a struggling newspaper."

Other commentators have been less charitable, one tartly observing that Jack "had become a cocky, opinionated and determined youth, with aggressive confidence in his own ability. He loved Ottawa with its maze of political grapevines, the atmosphere of the Press Gallery and the lobby and smoking room of the Russell Hotel." One doubts that the smoking room at the Russell Hotel was the main Ottawa attraction for the young editor. It was more likely the front parlour at 261 Maria Street.

The *Journal* published its first number on December 21, 1885. "The paper," biographer Murray Donnelly tells us, "was set up in a way that was typical of the times, with two outside columns of advertising on the front page and two columns of news in the middle. The two main items of news in the first issue were the Home Rule crisis in Ireland and the disastrous activities of a mad dog in New Jersey. The second page had more advertising and a romantic serial, and the third was the editorial page. The first editorial, called 'Is a General Election Pending?,' was the kind that editorial writers churn out when they have a space to fill and very little to say. However, the young editorial writer soon began to hit his stride, to enjoy expressing himself, and his writings over the next few months touch upon many of the themes he developed with such force over the next sixty years." Questions of national identity, Canada's place in the wider world and in the Empire, the importance of education and the need for Canadians to know and understand their own history—matters that were of deep concern to him

until the end of his life—were first touched on by the young editor
in the pages of the *Ottawa Journal* during those hectic months of
1885 and 1886.

In one editorial, for example, he complained that "our present
hole-in-corner politics, the senseless strife over issues not worth
ten minutes consideration, the unpatriotic and demagogic ap-
peals to prejudices of race and creed and section are preventing
far more effectually than the natural obstacles of which we hear
so much from pessimists, the welding together of different provinces and the unification of our Confederation into a stable and
strong nation." How little things change as the centuries roll on.

"After about five months of it," Jack would recall, "I had sense
enough to realize I was beyond my depth." The paper's circulation
was stuck at just over one thousand and financial disaster loomed.
Jack resigned, the *Journal* passing, eventually, into the hands of his
older friend from the *Montreal Star*, P.D. Ross, who bought a half
interest in the paper for $4,000, turning it, after many trying times
and much fancy financial footwork, into one of the nation's leading Conservative newspapers. It would survive well into the last
decades of the twentieth century.

Jack would make light of his failure in future years, but at the
time it must have been a great humiliation. The urge to remove
himself from the scene of his downfall was strong. For a moment
he seems to have contemplated forsaking journalism in favour of
a literary career in Chicago or New York, a course followed by
many Canadian writers in the late nineteenth century, including
his friend the poet Bliss Carman and his old friend from Montreal,
George Iles, who had settled in New York and was now working
in writing and publishing. Iles, in fact, urged him to hurry down
to New York and join the gang.

As much as he enjoyed journalism, Jack had not entirely for-
saken his old ambitions. The historian Frank Underhill, writing
in *Canadian Forum* in 1932, noted that "A little while ago, while

working through the files of *The Week*, the organ of Canadian intellectuals in the 1880s, I came across a tender ballad by J.W. Dafoe of Montreal. It was about a fair maiden who waited sadly by the seaside for the return of her beloved, who alas would never return, for the ocean waves had buried him. As an admirer and friend of Mr. Dafoe I shall never reveal the date of the issue of *The Week* in which that youthful effort lies hidden."

The poem was called "Down by the Sea" and was published in *The Week* in 1884, when Jack was 18, shortly after he had taken up his duties in the Ottawa Press Gallery for the *Star*, which also printed the poem in its columns. It is clearly the work of someone with very little experience of life, but a close acquaintance with contemporary rhyming verse in newspapers and popular magazines. The maiden waiting by the shore is a staple of the folk song and the popular ballad and Jack's effort is no worse than many, although want of a rhyme forced him to pair "kiss" with "I wis." Journalism had laid its hand on him, but he was still writing poems and occasionally publishing them. He had made literary friends, including William Henry Drummond, the author of the popular "Habitant" poems, and the poets Archibald Lampman and Duncan Campbell Scott, both civil servants in Ottawa. He may have been inspired, as well, by the thought that two of the major Canadian poets of an earlier generation—Charles Heavysege and Charles Sangster—had been journalists.

By 1885 Jack must have felt that international recognition was near when one of his poems was accepted for publication by *The Current*, a literary and political magazine produced in Chicago that had included among its contributors Charles G.D. Roberts, Joaquin Miller, Emile Zola, Lionel Tennyson, James B. Cable and Henry Ward Beecher. By this time the 19 year old poet had already met the girl he hoped to make his wife and from now on the poems he wrote would tend to be about love, as in his contribution to *The Current*:

SOMETIME

Sometime, sweetheart, our paths will cross again
And I will look once more into thine eyes,
And feel no more the sorrow and the pain,
While soft and sweet will sound thy sweet replies.

Sometime, dear heart, sometime, though ocean's foam
And mountains rise between us, we will meet,
Thy heart will find within my heart its home,
And all my bitter life will turn to sweet.

Gone were the horrors of war and the deep gloom of the young poet of romantic inclination and limited experience. Contentment loomed, always a danger to those yearning to write poetry.

In 1889, looking back, Jack spoke of his poems as being "youthful follies." He continued to write love poems for Alice, but they were for her eyes alone. "Since 1885," he would write, "my muse has been dumb, although some poems of mine were published a year or so later in some American publications. They were, however, old poems."

It may be that the closer he got to poets such as his friends Lampman, Carman and other outstanding figures of the period the more he realized the difficulty of writing true poetry. He may have come to see, as many others have done, that the laurel was not to be his. Prose would be his medium and journalism his trade.

Nevertheless, for a moment in those early months of 1886 Jack was sorely tempted to walk away from what seemed to be the ruins of his newspaper career and seek his fortune as a man of letters in the United States. The short story and the novel suggested themselves. Canada seemed to be in the doldrums. Perhaps the time had come to emigrate. Then he thought again. His friend Archie McNee, managing editor of the *Manitoba Free Press*, who was in Ottawa covering the Parliamentary session, offered him a job on the Winnipeg paper and Jack decided to try his luck in the

Last, Best West. Perhaps he saw Manitoba as a convenient place in which to lie low until the memory of his downfall became less painful. He may have envisaged a possible return to Ottawa as Parliamentary correspondent for the *Free Press* at some future date, putting him in position to resume his courtship of Alice Parmelee. Like many young Canadians of his time he may have been aware that the New West had become the Canadian land of opportunity, not only for him, but possibly for his parents, still in their forties, and his younger brothers and sisters. His father, who had been given a rough ride by his French Canadian co-workers in the lumber camps over the hanging of Louis Riel, badly needed a new start on a farm that might actually produce a crop. Jack knew next to nothing about the *Manitoba Free Press*, the province of Manitoba or the city of Winnipeg, but he had no doubt that he would make a go of it. The "cocky, opinionated" brat, it seems, was bruised, but not crushed. He packed his bags, stuffed a couple of books into his coat pocket and set off for the West with a light heart.

ESCAPE TO THE WEST

The Winnipeg that Jack saw when he stepped off the train from the East in early May 1886 was still recovering from the abrupt reversal of fortune that had followed the collapse of the great land boom which took place at the beginning of the decade, described by one observer as "the wildest sixteen months" in the city's existence. The announcement that the CPR would run its main line through Winnipeg had started a wild orgy of land buying and speculation in 1881. There were many losers and a few winners. Among the latter was the remarkable Big Jim Coolican, also known as "The Marquis de Mud," who presided over a land auction shack or "gambling hell" on muddy Main Street, quaffing champagne and allegedly selling a cool million dollars worth of overpriced real estate during one spectacular two-week period before prudently slipping out of town and over the horizon. "The growth of Winnipeg," one eastern magazine reported, "has been phenomenal... land on Main Street and the streets adjoining is held at higher figures than in the centre of Toronto, and Winnipeggers, in referring to the future, never make comparisons with any city smaller than Chicago." It was all over by April Fools Day 1882 and Winnipeg came down to earth with a bump.

By the spring of 1886 many still believed that the rising city at the edge of the great prairie would shortly become the Chicago of the North, but for the moment progress appeared to be more or less at a standstill. The population of the straggling, largely jerry-built town stood at around 20,000. Commercial activity was sluggish, but fervent optimism continued to animate civic and business leaders. Winnipeggers pointed proudly to the new city hall which had risen like a turreted gingerbread cake on Main Street close to the posh Leland Hotel, replacing an earlier civic edifice that had been pulled down just as it appeared about to totter and collapse. The wide streets were clogged with mud through which Red River carts still noisily passed and in which careless pedestrians sank up to the knees in sludge and horse manure if they left the duckboards.

Lieutenant Richard Scougall Cassals of the North-West Field Force, passing through the city on his way home from the unpleasantness of the North West Rebellion a year earlier, had been pleasantly surprised by the small city. After a guided tour, Cassalls and some fellow officers dined at Clougher's, "the swell Winnipeg restaurant" and later mixed with local military men at their club. "Winnipeg," he wrote in his diary, "we are all charmed with, the place bright and handsome, and the people most kind. The beautiful decorations (the arches are most fine) make everything look unwontedly gay now, but at any time the city must be goodly to look upon. Some surprisingly handsome churches and public buildings."

Jack had arrived in the city not knowing what to expect. What he discovered was a town in the process of transition. There were still plenty of old timber buildings, some not much better than shacks, along the main streets and there was a growing shantytown out on the Hudson's Bay Flats near the Red River, but good brick and stone buildings were also to be seen. Old Fort Garry was mostly a memory, but several impressive hotels, such as the Leland, Seymour House, the Queen's and the Clarendon, were welcoming visitors. Residential districts were beginning to spread onto the prairie where the air was sweeter. There were book shops, theatres, restaurants, tailor shops and well-stocked grocery stores, butcher shops, bakeries and general merchandise stores where imported goods were for sale. There was a university with real professors and a couple of church colleges. Street lighting was visible here and there and a few people had telephones. Trees were being planted. Friends such as George Iles had warned Jack that he would probably end up living in a mud hut—or worse. You had to be careful not to fall into the mud on Main Street and dogs and other animals left messes to soil your shoes on the foot path. It was a tough town after dark. There were bars along the downtown streets full of noisy and sometimes bellicose drunks, but the whorehouses were tucked discreetly away on the edge of town. Jack liked the look of his new home, the broad skyline and the covering of stars at night. He moved into a boarding house near the *Free Press* office on McDermot Avenue, nicknamed "Newspaper Row" because of nearby competing newspapers, and prepared to become a Winnipegger.

In the slowly reviving city Boosterism was in full bloom. A promotional booklet published later in 1886 bragged that "The history of Winnipeg, with its wonderful growth and marvellous progress, reads like a chapter from some work of romance." Under the rubric "Winnipeg To-Day" the authors continued their fantasia: "Its advancement has been of no ordinary character, but has in its rapidity and solidity outstripped every other city in the world. Ancient or modern times fail to furnish a similar example of sudden growth and permanent prosperity, and the metropolis of the Canadian Northwest to-day stands unapproachable in its supremacy." The size and number of the mosquitoes was not mentioned.

Business may have been in the doldrums, but, as Jack noted, Winnipeg "had no lack of newspapers; in the morning the *Free Press*; in the evening the *Sun*, the *Manitoban*, and the *News*. All were four-page papers. The page of the *Free Press* was the largest size possible and it was known as a blanket sheet." The *Manitoba*

Free Press, published both daily and weekly, had been started as a weekly in 1872 by John A. Kenny and William Fisher Luxton and had survived and expanded while many of its erstwhile rivals had run out of money and readers. In civic promotion material for 1886 the *Free Press* is described as "the finest newspaper property in the Northwest. The daily is an eight-column folio and the weekly edition is the largest newspaper in the Dominion, averaging from 20 to 24 pages and enjoying an immense circulation throughout Manitoba and the territories. The *Free Press* is Reform in politics, but is ever ready to support the interests of the Northwest in preference to party. The editor-in-chief, Mr. W.F. Luxton, is a prominent leader of the Reform party of Manitoba."

Luxton, who had earlier worked on newspapers in the Ontario towns of Goderich and Seaforth, had hatched his plan to start a Winnipeg newspaper in the late summer of 1872 around the time that riots halted the production of several city newspapers. Kenny had recently arrived from Ontario with $4,000 from the sale of a farm in his pocket which he was willing to invest in Luxton's project. We see in the pages of Alexander Begg's and Walter Nursey's day-to-day-year-to-year history *Ten Years in Winnipeg*, published in 1879, that Luxton had resigned his post as schoolteacher in August 1872. He was off to New York "for the purpose of purchasing the plant and material for his proposed paper."

He arrived back on the steamboat in late October with a $1,200 Taylor printing press. "On the 9th of November," Begg and Nursey reported, "the *Manitoba Free Press*, a new weekly literary creation, made its salutary bow and was ushered into existence with an advance specimen number. With the Reform banner nailed to the mast, it sailed into the somewhat turbid seas of political Manitoba an uncompromising advocate of Reform in politics and liberality in all things." The paper's official motto from volume one was "Freedom of Trade, Liberty of Religion, Equality of Civil Rights," although it was whispered by some that the real motto was "Give them our compliments and tell them to go to Hell." The paper soon published daily and weekly editions, subscribers paying 25 cents a week for daily delivery and $2.50 per annum for the weekly, which had a growing rural circulation. While rivals foundered, the *Free Press* prospered.

The former editor of the *Ottawa Journal*, now reduced, as Jack saw it, to the ranks, reported for duty to his new chief at the *Free Press* early in May 1886 and, on the strength of his experience in the press galleries at Ottawa and Quebec City, was assigned to cover the Manitoba Legislature. Jack looked around him with a sinking heart. Had he exiled himself to a remote and obscure backwater for six dollars a week? "Manitoba in those days," he would recall years later, "was to all appearances an insignificant province; one would say that nothing that could happen here politically could have repercussions outside of its boundaries. But in the six years I was there two issues of Dominion-wide importance engaged the attention of people and legislature. One was the final success of the long fight against the exercise by the Dominion government of its powers of disallowance for the purpose of preserving a railway monopoly in the province. The other was the breaking out of the Manitoba school question. These two controversies, which I saw develop from beginnings which seemed to be nothing more than a mere item in the day's news into nation-shaking causes, awakened in me a knowledge of the historic importance of events that may at first sight seem insignificant. You may write the report of an event and it goes into the paper—it is all in the day's work, to be forgotten. But later you may find that what you were dealing with was a turning point in the history of your country."

On the other hand, there were frequent occasions when it seemed that there was not enough news to fill the paper and Jack soon found that his duties were by no means confined to the lofty sphere of politics and the legislature. Staff members were expected to lend a hand on all reporting assignments from crime to the hotel beat, from writing pieces for the editorial page to reviews and reports on sporting events and Sunday sermons. Winnipeg was a tough town and even the church beat could be dangerous, as Jack reported in a letter: "I went to church to-night—to the Congregational church—and as a reward I fell over a boot-scraper at the door and hurt my ankle enough to give me an elegant limp for a few days. This is the reward of virtue. The rest of the evening I spent writing up the sermon."

George Ham, a veteran of the Winnipeg newspaper wars, recalling a slightly earlier era at the *Free Press*, described a situation that was still causing vexation in Jack's day: "The reporter's position was not, at all times, a very pleasant one, for on wintry days, when the mercury fell to forty degrees below zero and the telegraph wires were down and there were no mails and nothing startling doing locally, it was difficult to fill the *Free Press* with interesting live matter. A half dozen or so drunks at the police court only furnished a few lines, nobody would commit murder or suicide or even elope to accommodate the press, and the city council only met once a week." Sometimes the never-ending search for "live" news got the journalists into hot water. On one occasion, Jack recalled, the *Free Press* published a death notice that had been handed in. "Next day the 'corpse' turned up and made things lively at the office."

Jack threw himself into his work with enthusiasm, putting in long hours but saving time for reading and recreation. He joined the rowing club and tried out for a lacrosse team. He went for long walks and got to know the city. He eventually became an expert oarsman, a member of the Rowing Club, but, although strong and eager, he proved to be awkward on the field and had to settle for becoming secretary of the lacrosse team, after falling over his stick "like a chump." He was slow to make friends among his fellow journalists, possibly because he did not drink, but he was welcomed as a member by the town's several debating and conversation clubs, particularly by one called "The Non-Smokers Association" that met regularly to smoke cigars and pipes and to argue about literature and the issues of the day, Jack, as usual, the odd-man-out who did not smoke. Later in the year he would become a blanket-coated member of the St. George's snowshoe club, joining prominent businessmen, politicians and lawyers on bracing moonlight hikes along the Red and Assiniboine rivers and over the starlit prairie.

Shortly after his arrival in Winnipeg, Jack was faced with the problem of what to do about his family back in Ontario. The Dafoes were not doing well in Combermere. The farm had never supported the family and Cal and his oldest son Will had to find work in the lumber camps and on the railway to put food on the table and pay the bills. Cal was in debt and Jack received frequent requests for loans and other assistance. He had been sending money to help with the education of his brothers and sisters ever since he had left home. Now he proposed that his parents start again in the West. Early in the summer of 1886 he went with a land guide into newly opened territory in the south west corner of the province near the rising town of Killarney and filed for a homestead in his father's name to be taken up in the spring of 1887.

The family was delighted at the prospect of a new start in the West, although his mother was worried about the town's name. Killarney? Could it be a Roman Catholic town? Would Methodists be welcome? In a letter written from Bangor on 12 August 1886 she spoke of Cal poring over an old map of the West trying to locate their future home and about the possibility of living in a tent at first. The initial plan was that the Combermere farm would be taken over by her elder son Will and his wife, the difficult Roxey, and Jack's mother was worried by a suggestion that she might stay on with them until the new farm was ready. "For pity's sake," she wrote, "don't ask me to stay here after Roxey is mistress here."

She also wondered why Jack had not sent them any copies of the *Free Press*. His father, who had enjoyed reading his son's articles in the Conservative *Montreal Star* and the non-partisan *Ottawa Journal*, kept looking in the post box for a copy of the Liberal *Free Press*. "Do you think us such dreadful Tories that you have never sent us a paper?" his mother asked.

As excitement grew over the proposed move, Jack's father had a few questions of his own. Were there stones on the land? Was the village a Protestant one and what churches were there? The elder Dafoes, with their younger sons Teddy, Rance, Calvin and Wallace, with sister Maggie and her husband and child, arrived in Killarney in March 1887 and settled onto the new farm, relieved to find that there was a Methodist church nearby. In that first summer their crop was hailed out, fervent prayers notwithstanding.

As 1886 drew to a close Jack was still feeling intense pain over Alice Parmelee's letter rejecting his proposal of marriage. He knew he must try again, but when and how? The vast, empty wastes of the snow-covered Dominion stood between Winnipeg and Ottawa. As he plodded along the Red River with the men of the snowshoe club or contemplated another Saturday night alone in his draughty boarding house bed-sitting room he was painfully aware that Alice was far away, probably forgetting him as she played cribbage and danced with the young sparks of Ottawa.

Just before Christmas, Jack received an unexpected and surprising letter from Hugh Graham, the proprietor of the *Montreal Star*. Marked "Confidential," the letter contained a tempting offer: "I write to ask you if you will entertain an offer to come back to the *Star*, your first love, as a writing Editor and Parliamentary Correspondent. Mr. Ross leaves us in early January for the *Ottawa Evening Journal*, in which he has bought an interest. Mr. Dalby will succeed him. The next time the Managing Editorship is vacant you would have the first claim and no doubt you would have it offered you. My present ideas are to retire from business some of these years. To leave the paper in the hands of a Joint Stock Company, comprised only of trusted employees, selected from the Editorial, Business and Mechanical Departments, retaining a half interest for myself. If you should think well of coming on the staff, you would in all human probability be one of those to whom an opportunity would be offered."

For a blissful moment Jack must have felt like Christ in the wilderness being offered the kingdoms of the Earth. A job in Montreal with an assignment in Ottawa would put him close to Alice for purposes of courtship and, possibly, early marriage. He would occupy a commanding position in the *Star* organization with the prospect of further advantageous advancement. And he was just out of his teens.

And yet he paused. Was it all too good to be true? There were problems. The *Star* was a solidly Conservative paper and he was drifting more and more toward the Liberals. Would he really fit in? Hugh Graham had been a friend to him and was offering even closer favour, but at what price? Besides, he was moving his family to the West and he needed to be on hand to see them settled. It would be helpful to be planted closer to Alice, but the *Free Press* could be expected to send him to Ottawa eventually. His recent unhappy experience at the *Ottawa Journal* still made him wince. Was he ready for a comeback in the East or would he be wise to remain in Winnipeg, muck in, and devote a few busy years to becoming a better and more experienced newsman? Jack's reply to Hugh Graham has not survived, but the offer was not taken up. No bridges were burned, however, and a few years later, when Jack was in need of a job, Hugh Graham would prove to be a friend in need. Nevertheless, the young journalist, thinking twice, decided that the offer, splendid as it undoubtedly was, simply represented too much temptation, too soon.

In need of advice, Jack had been in touch with his friend P.D. Ross over the Graham offer, Ross commenting on the situation and offering a warning in a letter sent from the *Ottawa Journal* office on 19 January 1887: "Dear John, Your head is level, if red—there is no future for you on the *Star*—not even the future of honest work. Sincerity has no swing beneath the Grahams and you, like myself, could only be comfortable when feeling honest. I don't pretend that this is particularly to our credit, inasmuch as we were born honest and haven't made ourselves so (in fact, I think you have retrograded, being now a wretched Grit), but however it comes about, honest we are and have got to abide by it. Now honesty is the best policy to Hugh Graham only when it is the popular policy. He is to my mind one of the cleverest men in Canada and it is a loss to the country that he has not the vital and moral force which usually accompanies the ability of a self-made man. I was never comfortable on the *Star* on the ground above indicated and it has been a tremendous relief to me here to be able to go home at night without feeling that I am endeavouring to wag my tail vigorously when in reality it is very much between my legs."

The Ross comments notwithstanding, Jack was to retain a warm affection for his old chief that lasted until the end of his life. In his valedictory address in 1943 he looked back to the year 1885 and Graham's courage and devotion to public service in confronting a horrendous smallpox epidemic that swept the city of Montreal. "Returning to Montreal in the early summer of 1885," he recalled, "I speedily realized that a news story of great importance was being suppressed. The city was in the grip of a smallpox epidemic already well advanced. People suffering from the malady could be seen in the streets. But all the powers of the city, business and financial, were determined that nothing should be said about it. It would be bad for the tourist industry, it would keep trade from the city, and so forth and so on. Defying the great and powerful would be for the *Star* a risky business. But Hugh Graham took the bit in his teeth and one day he blew the story in good newspaper style, large headings, alarmist language and so forth. The indignation of the flouted powers was prodigious: the *Star* was threatened and the threats were not idle ones. But within a week the intelligence and public spirit of the city was mobilized, and during that whole terrible summer Graham, the *Star* and the group of citizens that rallied to his leadership were foremost in grappling with the emergency. The most strenuous methods had to be taken. There was compulsory vaccination. There were anti-vaccination riots—one was staged within fifty yards of the house where I roomed, its purpose being to take vengeance on an alderman for his activities in fighting the plague. The city was cut off from the rest of the continent; one could not get into it or out of it without being held up for vaccination, as I learned by personal experience. Before the epidemic ended some five thousand people died. That was to me a lesson in both the power and the duty of newspapers."

Having decided to remain in Winnipeg, Jack plunged into work, recreation and earnest self-improvement. "I am really getting a lot of books together," he observed, "a few now and a few again count up in a couple of years. And I don't buy them for their binding either for I am fairly familiar with the contents of every book on my shelves. It is about the only thing I am extravagant in. I cannot resist the temptation to buy a good book when I see it." His room at the boarding house had become his university where the oil lamp burned late even after a long, weary day chasing the news. "I have not had very much time for reading," he noted in a letter written in the late eighties, "but manage to get through a good deal during the week. Whenever I am in doubt what to take up to spend an hour I get my Shakespeare down and read one of his plays, and in this way I am furbishing up my knowledge of the great dramatist. When I was in Montreal I used to read a play of Shakespeare's every Sunday. Just at present I am running through Macaulay's *Life and Letters*. I ought really to re-read his History, which I have. It is just 10 years or a little more since I read it, but so extraordinary an impression did it make on my mind that I know it better than plenty of works that I read only last year. Carlyle's *Cromwell* is also down on the list and of Goethe I also intend to know something." He delved into popular works on science. He was reading poetry too: Tennyson was a favourite and Walt Whitman, Shelley and Browning were frequently consulted. He had read Ibsen. Novels by Thackeray, Dickens and Trollope were piled on his bedside table. Another frequently read volume was the collection of essays called *Dreamthorpe* by the Scottish poet Alexander Smith, a Victorian bestseller that Jack described as a work "that will always remain one of my favourite books." Sometimes he was too weary on a Saturday night to read: "I came in about half past nine and laid myself out for a few hours reading. In order to have lots of scope I picked out a dozen books or so and laid them on my table within my reach—Tennyson, Mrs. Browning, Thackeray's *Newcomes*, Whitman's *Specimen Days*, a bound volume of *Scribner's Magazine* and several cheap novels. I couldn't read any of them. An hour or so passed until I turned in and slept for about 12 hours."

He subscribed to Henry George's *Standard*: "It made me sad, as indeed it always does, for it shows from week to week the dark side of the shield. It brings home to one a sense of the pain of the world; of the suffering, of the despairing poverty which millions are, at least under existing circumstances, doomed to bear. I suppose it would be more comforting to hide our eyes to these grim realities, but only by facing them can we hope that some day the world will be able to mitigate these evils." Not for him the complacency and unquestioning satisfaction so often and so mistakenly attributed to the Victorians of his generation. When he looked about him he saw more questions than answers, more shadow than sunlight. "I am not an enthusiastic admirer of Carlyle," he wrote to his future wife in 1889, "He makes me tired with his eternal roaring against modernism and science as though the world were retrograding. I am no optimist. My heart bleeds for the pain, the sorrow, the misery, the suffering I see on every hand. There is no reason to doubt but what the average of happiness reaches a higher point every year, and yet the progress is so slow that it is enough to make one despair, and yet we must believe in progress."

While he polished up his education and studied the ideas of the age, Jack also took time to use the columns of the *Free Press* to strike a blow for struggling Canadian literature in the manner of young critics then, and now: "I am deep into the midst of an article for the Christmas Number. It is a few plain words to the Philistines of the Northwest on the claims to their support that Canadian literature has. The subject has a tendency to grow on my hands and I will have to keep it in reasonable limits or the Philistines aforesaid won't condescend to read more than the headlines."

He was learning fast. The variety of work that came his way at the *Free Press* helped to make him a more rounded and thoughtful journalist than he had been in Ottawa and Montreal. In the East he had started near the top. In Winnipeg he touched all the bases and went from strength to strength rapidly. He was filling in the gaps in his calendar of newspaper experience. During the next hundred years many young journalists would come to the *Free Press* to sharpen their talents before moving out into the wider world of newspaper work. Many of them would say that the *Free Press* was "the best journalism school in the country."

It certainly served that purpose for Jack. His tremendous energy was also a help. Fourteen or fifteen hour working days he took in his stride. He was always on duty and he enjoyed it so much that it hardly seemed like work. He had found his vocation.

THE GRAVEYARD OF JOURNALISM

Jack would be present at Clougher's restaurant in Winnipeg on
2 April 1888 when members of the city's newspaper fraternity
gathered to celebrate what some of them called "the graveyard of
journalism." There were men present at that Press Club reunion
dinner who could look back on almost 30 years of newspaper activity in the young prairie city. There were others present, including
Jack, who would help carry on the journalistic life of the city well
into the next century. In the chair that night in 1888 was William
Luxton who, with John A. Kenny, had launched the *Manitoba Free
Press* in 1872. One important old-timer was conspicuously missing from the company. William Coldwell, who had co-founded
the settlement's first newspaper, the *Nor'-Wester*, in November
1859, was indisposed and so an interesting memoir he had prepared for the occasion was read by a proxy to the gathering that
included, as well as Luxton, such Winnipeg news veterans as W.G.
Fonseca, George H. Ham, Walter Nursey, Stewart Mulvey, C.W.
Handscomb, E.A. Blow, Walter Payne, T.H. Preston, F.C. Wade
and a special guest, the highly popular United States Consul and
American spy, James Wickes Taylor, a former newsman himself.

Many Canadian cities have claimed the title, but few can rival
Winnipeg as "the graveyard of journalism." The *Free Press*, born
into an uncertain world in the nineteenth century, has endured
into the twenty-first, but the long road over which the paper has
travelled is littered with the bones of failed rivals. Looking back

at the carnage, one can only marvel at the optimism that marked those brave attempts to win the circulation wars. Winnipeg earned its reputation as a dangerous place in which to launch a newspaper when it was hardly big enough to support a single paper, let alone several.

To the younger men at the 1888 reunion dinner, the year 1859 must have seemed romantically remote; to older men such as Nursey and Ham who remembered Winnipeg as a collection of tottering, windswept shacks above the Red River, 29 years back was not much farther away than the day before yesterday. Many of the older men remembered William Coldwell as an active journalist. Coldwell himself was still in his fifties in 1888 and he would live on until 1907, but by the time the newsmen gathered at Clougher's restaurant his active days were over. Jack, in a letter to his future wife written early in 1890, commented on some recent Coldwell contributions made to the *Free Press* and told something of the veteran pressman's situation at that time: "Coldwell is the pioneer journalist of the North West, but he has been partially paralyzed for years. I have never seen him for he keeps to his home, but I have heard much of him as a very remarkable man. His occasional contributions to the press are certainly of much more than average ability." At another gathering in Winnipeg almost half a century later it was Jack, by then the grand old man of Winnipeg journalism, who would hold his audience spellbound with tales of the city's long and colourful newspaper history.

William Coldwell was born in England in 1834. After schooling in Dublin, he came out to Canada in 1854, finding work in Toronto on the *Leader* newspaper. In 1859 he and William Buckingham, a friend from the *Globe*, set out for the North West to start their own paper. Coldwell's own account of the journey, read at Clougher's restaurant in 1888, is a tale of adventure and comedy. To save money, Coldwell and Buckingham got their press and type at St. Paul and brought them in ox carts along the Crow Wing Trail to Red River. George A. Winship, an American from Minnesota, who came to the settlement later to serve as printer, described the press and printing materials obtained by Coldwell and Buckingham as "worn out stuff discarded by printers in St. Paul and St. Anthony. The Washington hand press was said to have been the original hand press from which the St. Paul *Pioneer* was printed in 1849. In the early fifties the *Pioneer* office was partially destroyed by fire and the press fell from the second storey into the cellar. It was recovered, patched up by a blacksmith and sold subsequently to the enterprising founders of the *Nor'-Wester*, together with a meagre assortment of type, galleys, rules, sticks and other things necessary for the publication of a weekly newspaper. When I looked upon this collection of old junk, noted the crippled condition of the press, the pied type on galleys and in the various cases and the chaotic state generally of the entire office, I was somewhat disconcerted. I saw several weeks clean up ahead of me before the regular edition of the paper could go to press. We got the type and some other things in fairly good shape, but the old press could not be improved much, and it was the source of much annoyance during my entire term of service."

While bringing all these oddments up to the Red River Settlement in 1859, the Coldwell-Buckingham expedition nearly came to grief when one of the oxen bolted, scattering type as it ran. The crossing of the Red Lake River nearly finished Coldwell. He was observed by a passerby at the ford with only his head and his stove pipe hat rising above the rushing stream.

Arriving at Red River the partners discovered that the scanty population of the settlement was not unanimous in its desire for a local newspaper. A few signed up for subscriptions, but there were others who would not be tempted. "The inevitable crank," Coldwell, recalled, "had to be encountered even in this remote part of the world, and accordingly in our canvass we met persons who assured us that they did not want the *Nor'-Wester*, because they knew more local news than we did. They were also afraid that if they supported one journal in their midst, soon there would be two, four or a score knocking at the door with a wide diversity of views to the great bewilderment and detriment of an innocent and confiding public! Each of these cranks left us minus twelve shillings sterling, and yet we were incorrigible."

Manitoba Provincial Librarian J.P. Robertson, in an article written for the Canadian Press Association in 1908, described the beginnings of journalism in the Red River Settlement: "The first issue of the *Nor'-Wester* is dated the 28th December, 1859, and was published at Fort Garry, a mere hamlet, yet the Chief Post of the Hudson's Bay Company in this country. It was a four-page weekly with quite a lot of advertisements, well selected Canadian and foreign news; its leaders, too, were ably written, and had much to do with the early development of Manitoba and its subsequent transfer to the Dominion of Canada."

Buckingham soon grew weary of the struggle and returned to the East where he enjoyed a distinguished newspaper career at the *Stratford Beacon* and as secretary and biographer to Prime Minister Alexander "Sandy" Mackenzie. Coldwell carried on, assisted at various times by his brother-in-law James Ross, the gifted son of fur trader and historian Alexander Ross, and by Dr. John C. Schultz, who would later play a dramatic role against Louis Riel during the Red River Rebellion, serve as a senator and, in his old age, preside as Lieutenant-Governor of Manitoba. After an office fire in 1864 Coldwell gave up and sold out to Schultz, returning to Toronto where he worked for a time at the *Globe*.

George Winship, who served as chief printer at the *Nor'-Wester* under the Schultz ownership, recalled in a memoir published in 1928, that "The bulk of the circulation was in the settlements north of the town, and up the Assiniboine to Portage la Prairie." The position of editor was held briefly at this time by R.P. Meade.

"He was," Winship remembered, "a good writer and a man of considerable culture, but lacked initiative and force; was devoid, in fact, of the newspaper instinct. Too much space was given to heavy editorials, discussing imperial and dominion politics; and too little to local and Northwestern news. Among the innovations of the time was the dating of the paper from Winnipeg instead of from Fort Garry; and I remember how Meade insisted on spelling Winnipeg 'Winnepeg' and how we printers were equally as insistent upon using an 'i' in the second syllable, instead of 'e.' Of course, when the proof was returned to us for corrections, we made it, but as a general thing our version of the proper spelling of Winnipeg received popular endorsement." And so, thanks to the power of the press, Fort Garry became "Winnipeg" and not "Winnepeg."

Coldwell was back at the end of the decade to start a new paper, *The Pioneer*, but, reaching the settlement just in time for the disturbances of 1869-70, he was forbidden by Louis Riel to continue his project. The astute Coldwell sold his printing equipment and sat tight until the arrival of the Wolseley expeditionary force from Canada and the hasty departure of Riel.

His next venture, undertaken with *Globe* correspondent William Cunningham, was the weekly *Manitoban*, launched in 1870. All went well until 1872 when election night rioters went on a rampage and put three newspapers—the old *Nor'-Wester*, the *Manitoban* and Joseph Royal's *Le Metis*—out of business. The *Manitoban* revived, surviving another two years, when it was merged with the *Standard* under the formidable Molyneux St. John, the *Standard*, in turn, being devoured by the *Free Press*. It had been a strenuous life and Coldwell's health soon failed him. "After me," he told the diners at Clougher's in 1888, "came the deluge of newspapers and all things became new."

In a letter written to Alice Parmelee in August 1889 Jack tells of discovering some interesting old newspapers in Winnipeg: "The other day in the provincial library I ran across bound volumes of the old *Nor'-Wester* issued here early in the sixties when the Red River Settlement was a little oasis in the midst of barbarism separated from civilization by 500 miles of prairie infested by warlike Sioux. It was a very good paper, although it told its readers of the death of the Prince Consort, the great battles of the Civil War, etc. about a month after their occurrence."

In a write-up of the 1888 reunion dinner in the *Free Press*, the reporter, E.A. Blow, noted that "The toasts list was brief. 'The Queen' was the only formal toast. In another circumstance the dinner was widely different from every other dinner that has been held for many years. The venerable old chestnut 'For He's a Jolly Good Fellow' was tabooed. One unlucky wight tried to start it early in the evening, but he was suppressed by a storm of groans." A solemn hush fell upon the room, however, when the toast to "Winnipeg newspapers" was proposed. To many in the room this was a moment to shed a tear to lost endeavour as the sorry list of casualties was read out.

In those far-off days you could start a newspaper with an investment of a few hundred dollars and after 1870 many ambitious newspapermen set out from Eastern Canada with a modest nest egg and a large dream about getting in on the ground floor of journalism in the expanding Canadian West. P.G. Laurie tried and failed with his *News Letter* in the early 1870s, although he later found success in Saskatchewan. Stewart Mulvey launched the paper he called *The Liberal* and watched it sink in 1871. W.G. Fonseca's *Daily Herald* lasted two weeks, Captain G.F. Carruthers's *Manitoba Gazette* had a year's run in 1872 while Alexander Begg's *Trade Review* survived for less than a year. There was another *Nor'-Wester*, a *Weekly Standard*, another *Daily Herald*, a *Manitoba Telegraph*, and Henry Clarke's *Gazette*. All failed, as did the comic weekly *Quiz* and C.R.Tuttle's *Times*. George Ham's *Tribune* went under and there was another

Manitoban, a *Morning Call*, Amos Rowe's *Daily Times*, the *News*, the *Daily Sun*, *The New Sun*, the *Daily Manitoban*, yet another *News*, *The Manitoba Daily Sun* and the *Morning Sun*. "All these," Blow reported, "excepting the *Free Press* and the two last mentioned, have passed into the happy land where sheriffs are unknown."

Several of them, in fact, passed into the jaws of the *Free Press*, including, in 1888, the latest *Manitoban*, which had become the *Morning Call*. "Later," Jack recalled in old age, "it absorbed *The Sun* and for five weeks it was the monarch of all it surveyed." The FP, in the years to come, would have long-term rivals such as Sanford Evans's *Telegram* and R.L. Richardson's *Tribune*, but in 1888 it appeared that Luxton's *Free Press* was set to crush all comers.

"At that time," Jack recalled years later, "Winnipeg appeared to be the Mecca of many of the most lively newspaper men in Canada. They flocked in and after a short stay a good many went out; some stayed, perhaps because they didn't have the price of a ticket." Among them was the humorist John R. Cameron who helped print the first issue of the *Free Press* in 1872 and later wrote a column called Noremac's Nonsense, W.E. MacLellan who, for a time, wrote partisan editorials for both the Liberal *Free Press* and the Conservative *Manitoban*, R.T. Preston, later owner of the *Brantford Expositor*, Fred C. Wade who left newspapering to become a lawyer, Albert Horton, afterwards editor of the Senate Hansard, A.C. Campbell, afterwards editor of the House of Commons Hansard and the popular freelancer R.K. Kernighan, "The Khan of Khanada." A number of early journalists came West with the Wolseley Expedition in 1870 and after the departure of Riel decided to stay on. The first news editor of the *Free Press*, Jack Cameron, came to the settlement with the troops as a sergeant. Molyneux St. John, came to Red River as a war correspondent in 1870 and decided to stay on, briefly editing the *Standard* newspaper and, much later, the *Free Press*. Another who came with the soldiers was Robert Cunningham who arrived as representative of the *Globe*, staying on as partner to William Coldwell.

Among the itinerant journalists, Jack would remember, "the most notable was Ed Farrer, who for a short time was editor of the *Times*. In many ways Farrer was the most remarkable journalist that Canada had ever seen. He was a man of extraordinary talent as a controversialist. It was a matter of record that he had written campaign literature for both parties at the Dominion elections in 1882. It was reported that he was once seen wandering about in the early dawn and that he explained that he had been up all night trying to figure out how he could answer his own case for the other side."

Farrer, an Irishman who was alleged to have studied for the priesthood in Rome, worked for a number of Canadian newspapers and had a profound influence on the development of Canadian journalism as a commentator independent of party. He was editor of the *Toronto Mail* in 1885, also serving for two years as editor of the *Globe*. He was to play a sinister role in John A. Macdonald's last campaign in 1891 when he was accused of involvement in a plot to break up Confederation and effect the annexation of Canada by the United States.

His sojourn in the West was brief, but memorable. Even in hard-drinking Winnipeg, Farrer's heavy boozing provoked comment and admiration. He had also upset local Conservatives as editor of Amos Rowe's *Times*, supposedly a Conservative organ, by vigorously attacking Tory policies. In a letter to his father the prime minister, Hugh John Macdonald, a Winnipeg resident, complained about Farrer's treatment of the party and reported that local Conservatives we talking of starting a new Tory paper. Amos Rowe and his editor soon parted company and Farrer returned to the East to create further disturbances.

Perhaps the most colourful character at the 1888 reunion dinner was the popular wit and raconteur George H. Ham, later described by Jack as "a man of extraordinary charm and humour, with a marvellous capacity for clever, instinctive impromptu and repartee." It was George Ham, on the operating table for emergency surgery, who turned to the attending surgeon and remarked, "Well, doctor, you can take my appendix, but please leave me my table of contents."

In a letter of 1890, Jack painted a brief word picture of the eccentric newsman: "He is a typical careless and light-hearted Bohemian who in his 43 or 44 years of life has probably worried less than I have in not much over half that time. He has many good points about him; the only drawback to him is that he isn't at all particular about the company he keeps—anything from a tramp printer to the Governor-General would do and he is equally at home with either. He is very clever and should have made a much greater success in life than he has."

George Ham arrived in Winnipeg on the steamboat International in 1875 "with four dollars in my pocket, ten of which I owed." It took him a week to land a job on the *Free Press* as a printer, but soon he was, as he reported in his memoirs *Reminiscences of a Raconteur*, "city editor, telegraph editor, news editor, reporter, proof reader and exchange editor."

Ham, born in Trenton, Canada West, in 1847, began his career as a boy journalist on the *Whitby Chronicle*, where he learned to set up type and got down the rudiments of shorthand. Later he would try storekeeping and insurance and he served as a sailor on the Great Lakes until seasickness put him on shore, but newspaper work kept calling him back. In fact, in those early days at the Free Press the few staff members were expected to do every kind of work, from setting type and sweeping out the office to writing stories, running the press and delivering the paper to subscribers.

"It would be a mistake to imagine," Ham later wrote, "that the Winnipeg of the early '70s was a city of angels. It is a regrettable fact that some, if not many, of its leading citizens may fairly be described as otherwise." Nevertheless, there was always a scramble to find enough real news to fill the four-page paper. The big local news story of that era was the arrival of the first locomotive, the famous Countess of Dufferin, by river on a barge towed by the Kittson Line's stern-wheeler Selkirk in 1877. The *Free Press* offered extensive reports on the engine's progress along the Red River and gave a dramatic account of the flotilla's arrival at Winnipeg. Ham, who would later be CPR publicity chief, realized then that the railway would be the making of Winnipeg and the West—and possibly the making of him.

When the land boom came in 1881-82, George Ham was in the thick of it: "A lot if us boarded at the Queen's Hotel, then run by Jim Ross, at whose table a quiet coterie sat." It is difficult to imagine a "quiet coterie" that included the ebullient George Ham, who was always the natural centre of any group in which he found himself. Champagne flowed at the Queen's during those brief, heady days of the boom—sometimes in the bar, sometimes in the bathtub— but when it all ended Ham stoically shrugged off his hangover and went back to work. The "quiet coterie" sobered up. Moving out of the Queen's, Ham settled into a rented house off South Main Street, but all was not well. The house, he complained, was full of ghosts that kept him awake at night with their loud moaning. On certain nights murky water rose noisily in the basement.

In 1879 Ham had left the *Free Press* to start his own paper, the Tribune, but the paper failed, Ham remarking that he had "contributed to the list of busted newspapers." His subsequent career in Winnipeg was busy and varied. He worked for the *Times*, where he became a bosom pal of Ed Farrer, and for other papers as they rose and fell. He covered the North West Rebellion of 1885 for the *Globe*, was for several years a Winnipeg alderman and for a time held the post of Registrar of Land Titles, leaving a deputy in charge while he carried on his newspaper work. By 1890, however, he had lost his sinecure and was facing hard times.

Jack lured him back to the *Free Press* temporarily in 1890 and hoped to make the appointment permanent, but after serving the FP in the Ottawa Press Gallery for a few months he was carried off by Sir William Van Horne to be head of publicity for the CPR, a job he held until the end of his long life in the late 1920s. Ham, a popular figure who hobnobbed with film stars and politicians, was immortalized in verse at the Ottawa Press Gallery Dinner in 1919: "God save the CPR, / Ingine to Parlour Car. / Save the CP! / Send them some more George Hams, / Soften newspaper slams, / Ward off the peoples' damns, / Save the CP!"

He became a familiar figure on trains and in hotels across America, always the life of the party, the focal point of any crowd, but a sad figure at the end when, years into the twentieth century, Jack met him in a parlour car on the train running between Ottawa and Montreal and reported to Alice that "He is a lonely old man, still making a bluff at appearing gay and light-hearted." It had been a long journey.

LEFT: Annette Parmelee at the end of the 1870s, about to begin her newspaper career at the *Montreal Star*. RIGHT: William Grannis Parmelee, father of Annette and Alice, as he began his career in the Dominion civil service at Ottawa in 1876.

The young John Wesley Dafoe in 1883 at the time he played undercover detective for *The Star.*

Jack as a teen-aged Ottawa gallery correspondent, 1884.

LEFT: Alice Parmelee in her late teens, as first seen by Jack in 1884.
RIGHT: Jack's grandfather, the old Chartist John Elcome, pictured about
the time he emigrated to Canada in 1857.

The three younger Parmelee sisters in 1889. Left to right Elizabeth, Julia and Alice.

Cal Dafoe and his wife Mary Elcome Dafoe, right, with the formidable
Aunt Aggie Elcome and Jack's young cousin Edna Elcome, 1880s.

Jack ready to make one more attempt to win Alice's hand, 1889.

The wedding photo by Notman and Son, Montreal, 1890.

The editor of the *Family Herald* and *Weekly Star,* Montreal,1895.

"At Last I feel that I have come into my kingdom." Editor of the *Manitoba Free Press*, 1901.

The Dafoe children in their new home in Winnipeg, 1902. BACK ROW: Ted and Mary Alice. FRONT ROW: Marcella, Elizabeth, Dorothy and Jack.

On the front steps of 509 Spence Street, Winnipeg, 1903. BACK ROW: Jack, Elizabeth and Mary Alice. FRONT ROW: Dorothy and Marcella.

The editor of the *Free Press* in his office,1920s. (This is the picture that shows how he looked for much of the rest of his life.)

Saving gasoline during the Second World War, the *Free Press* carriage rolls over the Assiniboine River. The editor occasionally collected grandchildren along the way.

Members of the Rowell-Sirois Royal Commission prepare to submit
the report, Ottawa, 1940. J.W. Dafoe standing second from left,
Dr. Sirois seated.

Brenda and Christopher Dafoe enjoy a chat with grandpa in his study, 1943.

ALICE GOES WEST

In the summer of 1887 Jack learned that Alice's parents would be stopping off in Winnipeg for a few days on their way to Vancouver where Mr. Parmelee had business to attend to in his capacity as Dominion Commissioner of Customs. He arranged to be on the platform at the station when the train arrived and he made himself useful to them during their stay, taking Mrs. Parmelee on a three-hour carriage tour of the city while her husband attended to government business. The Parmelees put up at the Queen's Hotel, Jack dropping by for a chat with Mr. Parmelee and, possibly, a game of cribbage. The next day they visited a Japanese shop and the Hudson's Bay store on Main Street. It was a quick visit and they were soon off. Jack sent them on their journey to the far West, no doubt, with a request to be remembered to their daughter Alice when they returned to Ottawa.

At Christmas that year, as a follow-up, he sent Alice a card signed only "From Your Friend," trusting the Winnipeg postmark to give her a strong hint about the identity of the sender.

In a letter to Alice in April 1889 he explained himself: "About that Christmas card. When I sent that I hoped to go East for the following Parliamentary session and while I wanted to remind you of my existence and turn your thoughts toward me a little bit, I did not want to alarm you and make you distant and hard to approach when I arrived." In the event, someone else was sent to

Ottawa to cover the session while Jack suffered on in Winnipeg, wondering if he would ever see her again.

In the summer of 1888 Jack picked up a Vancouver newspaper one day and saw that a "Mr. and Miss Parmelee" had recently left the west coast city for the East after a tour that had taken them to Vancouver Island and as far afield as Forest Grove, Oregon, where they had visited relatives.

Could it be Alice or was it one of her younger sisters, Bess or, possibly, Julia? "I was a greatly agitated young man," he would later tell Alice. "I went down to the station but found from the conductor that you had passed through the previous day. I came uptown and realized that I would go east the following winter and try, try again. But I never had any doubt but that it was you whom I had missed seeing. I *knew* it was you."

It *was* Alice and it was a trip that she would remember for the rest of her long life, enchanting her grandchildren deep into the twentieth century with tales of that wonderful and uncomfortable train journey across the empty prairies and through the mountains to the Pacific shore.

A journey across the nation on the new transcontinental railway was a tremendous undertaking in 1888. Much of the West was still unsettled, the Rebellion on the Saskatchewan was a near memory and most of the great Western plains remained unplanted and unfenced. A journey to the West came under the heading "Great Adventure." People were not used to long voyages by rail. It all took some getting used to. The constant swaying of the cars and the chanting of the wheels made Alice feel unwell. An early diary entry reads "I got quite ill just after dinner and cast up my accounts."

There were great compensations, however. Interesting things were passed as the train puffed along: the beautiful shore of Lake Superior, old Fort William, seemingly endless forests and miles of golden buttercups along the right-of-way. They stopped briefly at

Winnipeg to take on supplies and passengers and then continued west. It was high summer and the great prairie was an ocean of swaying grass and wildflowers as far as the eye could see. Alice got off the train at Brandon to pick some of the brilliant flowers and nearly got left behind. Farther West, through the Cypress Hills and near Maple Creek, there were heaps of buffalo bones among the flowers and bands of Indians passing on horseback. Thoughts of Hannah Dustin must have passed through her mind. She and her father read books, played euchre and drank lemonade as the train trundled through the vast and largely empty landscape. At stops along the way they bought buffalo horns and skulls to carry away as souvenirs. The chatted with Indians and found them far more interesting than many of the dull people they knew back in Ottawa. They were fascinated by the prairie dogs that stood on their hills watching intently as the train passed by. Occasionally antelope were sighted racing the train over the rolling land. And there were flowers everywhere, "very thick and so many colours— rose, pink and white, bluebells and sunflowers," as she recorded in her journal. No live buffalo were to be seen, only heaps of dry bones along the rail line waiting to be carted away for fertilizer. One morning they looked out from the train and saw a large wolf trotting along the plains.

During a stopover at the small village of Calgary a Chinese man with a long pigtail and a pointed hat came to collect the laundry and later everybody was annoyed when the train passed Banff at three in the morning when they were asleep.

When they woke up there were mountains topped with snow all around them. They sped through tunnels and along narrow cliffs, expecting to topple over at any moment. "We keep crossing bridges" she recorded in her diary. A CPR man told them that they would have to cross 1,249 more before they got to Vancouver. "We are up from the river bed thousands of feet," she wrote, "and then we look up and see the mountains towering above us.

I never saw such scenery!" The view, in fact, induced a feeling of great solemnity, almost like that experienced at a funeral. She had never imagined anything as spectacular as this. A train man regaled them with stories of coaches that had plunged off the rails and into the abyss.

Years and years later, when she was almost 90, Alice would take a final journey west to the Pacific on the CPR. The prairie portion of the trip was then quite different, with towns, cities and grain elevators along the way and huge farms where the vast fields of grass and wildflowers had once been. She could close her eyes and see it as it had been in 1888, a memory that seemed almost close enough to be real. When they passed into the mountains she opened her eyes and saw that there time had stopped still, all was as it had been and she was once more a young woman on one of her life's first great adventures. Years later, in 1930, she had flown in an aircraft from Paris to London, but that rail journey when she was 21 would always remain the greatest travel adventure of her life. It gave her a vision of the vastness of Canada that never faded.

Finally, on that summer journey of 1888, the Parmelees, father and daughter, arrived in the very new and exceedingly small city of Vancouver. It was, she noted, however, "larger than Brandon" and had grown up very quickly, having been burned to the ground two years before. "We went to the Leland Hotel, just facing the bay. A lovely view from the gallery. A large Japanese steamship in, the cargo not yet discharged. From the hotel steps we can see snow-covered mountains and one peak breaks into two summits which are exactly alike and resemble two crouching lions. Across the bay is a little Indian village, the buildings all pure white, which makes it look very pretty across the water." The air was brisk and bracing and it all looked like a new world.

They went deep into Oregon and she saw her cousins at Forest Grove and she was sick on the boat going over rough water to Vancouver Island. Then it was time to make the homeward journey.

Was she thinking of Jack as the train approached Winnipeg on the journey east? Would he be waiting at the station as he had been when her parents arrived a year earlier?

The train finally stopped at Winnipeg to collect mail and put off and take on passengers. Jack was not on the platform. He would be a day late getting to the station. Perhaps she was relieved or possibly she felt a rush of disappointment as the train left the city behind and still no Jack on the platform. We can only speculate. What we do know is that she sent him a Christmas card later that year signed with the words "For My Friend." Jack was amazed when he got it. Had his luck finally changed?

Early in 1889 he was given the assignment he had been dreaming of—covering the Parliamentary session in Ottawa for the *Free Press*. He packed his bag and caught the train for the East with his heart in his mouth and his fingers crossed.

CHANGING HER MIND

Jack had a bad case of the shakes when he arrived in the East early in January 1889 to cover the Parliamentary session for the *Manitoba Free Press* and to renew, if he could, his courtship of Alice Parmelee. His accustomed air of boundless self-confidence had evaporated in the frosty emptiness between Winnipeg and Ottawa. His plan to present himself at the Parmelee's new residence at 128 Slater Street suddenly seemed to be the height of folly. "I was not happy then and my imaginings were not very bright," he would later tell Alice. "I thought that perhaps you had forgotten me to all intents and purposes. Perhaps I was bound on a fool's errand. I had a big struggle before I could pluck up the courage to go around on the night of my arrival and when I finally did present myself at your door I was in as agitated a condition as I ever expect to be in. When you came through the door and shook hands with me I dare say I seemed cool enough, but I did not feel that way. I can remember you so well. You were wearing a blue dress and seemed much the same as when I bade you goodbye three years before, except that you had grown so much dearer to me."

"I had to appear," he later recalled "merely as an old friend renewing acquaintance and a few formal words were all I could say." Mr. Parmelee, at least, welcomed him with open arms. Their cribbage games and conversations were resumed as if Jack had been away only a few weeks instead of years. The returned suitor, however, remained a wallflower when the dancing began and his relationship with Alice tottered on a friendly but formal footing. His attempts to move closer to her were unsuccessful. He got skates and went to a carnival on the Rideau rink in the hope of seeing her, but she failed to appear. He put on a dress suit and attended a conversazione on natural history that he felt certain she would attend. She wasn't there. He invited her to accompany him to a recital given by the celebrated Canadian soprano Emma Albani. She declined. He haunted the Ottawa home of Alice's sister Annette and her husband Allan Ingalls, hoping for a private chat if she happened to come by. She did appear on a fateful Sunday afternoon, but she brought her mother with her. "A sight of you, even across Parliament Square," he would later confess, "was an event to me." These sightings, as it turned out, were to be fairly frequent because Alice, having passed the civil service exam, was now working as a Dominion Civil Servant, assisting in the sugar testing lab at the Department of Customs.

In a letter to Alice written a few months later he would describe his torment in that cold January: "I did a great deal of thinking and musing during the first few weeks in Ottawa. I don't think you were absent from my thoughts for an hour. I gave perfunctory attention to debates and political sensations, but I thought only of when I should see you again. I did not like to intrude myself on your father's house unduly, but I could not keep away more than a week at a stretch. During the first week or so I was frightfully blue. I don't know why, but I thought that you did not care for me in the least. I was as near despair as I ever expect to be, but I set my teeth and said 'I'll see this thing through if it breaks my heart. And after a week or two I began to buck up courage. I began to fancy you were kinder. We said very little, as you know, but I fancied that you were just a little interested. It was your eyes that gave me hope. Some nights they were very tender and I went home feeling very elated. I had my spells of doubting, but I never faltered in my intention of having it out. When I went up to Belleville to see my cousins I said 'When I get back to Ottawa I'll stand or fall.' The following Sunday I went to Annette's and as you know met your mother and you. Did nothing tell you that our fate was at hand?"

He had braced himself for a possible meeting with Alice at the Ingalls house that Sunday, March 24 1889, saying to himself, as he later recalled, "I'll do it today and if I can't speak to her I'll write to her." But when he got there he found not only Alice but her mother, and Annette's children and Annnette herself. No opportunity to fall to his knees and speak in the approved Victorian fashion presented itself. It was an awkward afternoon. Conversation stumbled along. Jack, while amusing the babies by flashing a light off a hand mirror onto the wall, accidentally shone the light directly into Alice's eyes, apologizing profusely and feeling foolish. Finally Alice and her mother took their leave. Jack let them get a head start and then started off on his own miserable walk home.

That night he sat down at his desk in the Press Gallery and wrote his second proposal letter, which has survived in the family records. "My Dear Miss Parmelee," he began, "The time approaches when I must return to Winnipeg, but I cannot bring myself to do that without bringing up a matter of much moment to me. I had but one purpose in coming east this winter: to see you and to say to you that I love you with all the affections of my heart." Acknowledging that he had tried and failed before, he continued: "I can only hope as I have hoped for many years that perhaps you were not altogether indifferent. Men are presumptuous in matters which mean so much to them. And so my dear I put my fate in your hands. On your answer will depend certainly the happiness and, I also believe, the success of my life. Will you give me the right to love you, to cherish you forever? Will you be my wife?"

Seemingly endless hours of agony followed the dispatch of the proposal letter. Big things were doing in the House of Commons on Monday and Tuesday as the members debated the controversial "Jesuit Estates" bill, but in the Press Gallery Jack sat like a man under an enchantment. The disposition of the Jesuits' ancient Quebec lands meant nothing to him. To his ears, the debate was like the buzzing of flies. Finally, late on March 26, two days after he had sent his letter of proposal, a reply was delivered to him in the Gallery. While the politicians droned on he read Alice's note: "Dear Mr. Dafoe, Forgive me for not answering you at once. I wanted time to think carefully that I might be true to myself and to you. I do not, and believe I never shall, love you in the way you wish. I know that having said that I have said all you wish to know, but I want to tell you that I cannot but be very proud that you should so care for me. The thought that you have cared will always be a help to my better self—for you must never be ashamed of it, although I can but hope that sometime soon you will find the ideal woman whom you have loved and mistakenly believe you have found in me. God bless you and grant you a happy as well as that noble thing a useful life." The letter was signed "Your sincere friend, Alice Parmelee."

"March 27 1889 was without doubt the hardest day I ever put in," Jack would admit in a letter to Alice written exactly a year later. "I got your letter on the evening of March 26 and it stunned me so that I don't think I fully realized until next day what a thorough wreck it had made of my plans. But the next day was one of unreserved darkness. On the morning of the 28th I began to look at the thing with saner eyes and was busy trying to devise some way of communicating with you before I left Ottawa when I got your father's note asking me to meet him. That revived my hopes still further and after I had a conversation with him my old hopes seemed to revive. He did not say much, told me I had better see you personally and then put me through a series of questions which delighted me beyond question because they made it clear to me that he expected to have me for a son-in-law. He said I could come down and see you any evening and I wanted to say 'tonight' but I could not come because I had promised to help Mr. Campbell with the Jesuit debates and so I had to fix the following evening—but how interminable seemed the hours of next day! I thought half past seven would never come. Meanwhile I had a dozen fervent speeches prepared, but when I came through the door they all went through the window and I could scarcely say a word. But you were quite as badly frightened as I was."

Alice had been overwhelmed by second thoughts almost as soon as she had sent the letter of rejection to Jack. At a loss about what to do to retrieve the situation, she had appealed to her parents. Mr. Parmelee, ever the practical man of business, sat down and wrote Jack a note suggesting a chat: "Dear Mr. Dafoe, I am told that you are intending to leave for Winnipeg very shortly. I would like to see you a moment before you go. Could you find it convenient to call either at the office during the day or at home during the evening?" That letter did not say much, but Jack saw at once that it changed everything. Deep gloom gave way to sunshine.

Later, when all their problems had been more or less sorted out, Alice would look back wistfully to that hectic few days in March 1889: "I have a great affection for that letter you wrote that day, but I do think it is too bad that circumstances cheated me out of having a proper regulation proposal from you by word of mouth. I think I shall have to get you to show me some day how you would have done it had not mother been with me that day."

After his return to Winnipeg, Jack received a letter of apology from Alice's mother for her apparent coldness to him during his time in Ottawa. "I know it was not your fault," she wrote, "that you did not get a chance to see me alone before leaving Ottawa and I assure you I had hard work to give you the chance to see

Alice alone as our house you know is always so full of company. I am afraid that you did not find me either very friendly or hospitable this time you were in Ottawa before I learned of Alice's feelings towards you. I thought it best for you both to see each other as little as possible if she did not care more for you than she did formerly. However when I understood her change of feelings I tried to make amends for any seeming coldness that I had shown. As for my objecting to you as a member of the family, I cannot: I never have heard one word against you and I shall try to make you feel like one of the family. You must know it is very hard for both Mr. Parmelee and myself to part with our dear little daughter, but we wish to do what is right for her happiness and I know of no one I should prefer over you." Misunderstandings were soon cleared up and Jack and Mrs. Parmelee remained warm friends until her death in 1899.

Even before the engagement had been officially announced, Jack got the impression that others were aware that something momentous was afoot. "I suppose," he would later confide in a letter to Alice, "that Annette had a pretty shrewd suspicion that you and I had been coming to some mutually agreeable arrangement. That last afternoon we walked out there I noticed an amused look in her eyes as though she were reading us through and through and knew exactly in what a flutter our hearts were. If such a thing is possible it will add an additional pleasure to my wedding you to know that it will make Annette really my sister; we have been such staunch friends for so many years."

In keeping with the popular Victorian custom of carefully avoiding the impression of unseemly eagerness to mate by opting for an extended engagement, the Parmelee-Dafoe nuptials were set for June 1890. With a full year of emotional torture and loneliness ahead of them, Jack prepared to return to Winnipeg while Alice contemplated the prospect of another full year testing sugar in the Customs Department lab in Ottawa. They could have

spared themselves the agony by appealing to the nearest clergyman or calling on a justice of the peace. They were, after all, an
up-to-date couple—they had both read Ibsen and George Eliot—
but, after all, the year *was* 1889 and they were living in Ottawa.

The fact of the matter was that they hardly knew each other.
Jack and Alice's sister Annette had been regular correspondents
since 1884. Only four letters had passed between Jack and Alice,
two written proposals of marriage from Jack to Alice and two letters of polite rejection from Alice to Jack. Each had sent the other
an unsigned Christmas card. Until March 1889 they had never
been in a room together in which others were not present. They
had never danced. They had never been on a date, other than being
part of a family group that had watched a debate from the public
gallery at the House of Commons. Jack had worshipped her from
afar and his first letter of proposal had taken Alice completely by
surprise. And yet she had noticed him and kept him in her mind
during the years in which he had been absent in Winnipeg. Perhaps
she had thought of him as Annette's interesting friend. Perhaps
she had noticed his friendship with her father. Now, by some mysterious means they were engaged to be married. They had a year to
start getting to know each other. Their courtship would take place
largely by post. Jack set the pace by writing one, sometimes two,
letters a day. They began as standard love letters, with flowery
phrases and galumphing compliments, but after a few lines the
ardent author would seem to tire of the rhetoric and branch out
into more general topics. He would discuss books he was reading,
poetry he liked, plays he had seen in one of the busy Winnipeg
theatres. He would speak of lacrosse and rowing and of the prairie landscape that he was coming to love. He spoke of his work
and the men he worked with. He wrote about his childhood and
his incomplete education. He wrote, as well, about what he was
learning about himself: "I don't expect the world to be all sunshine. I take life too seriously for that. And I am afraid you will

find me rather easily depressed, but I hope to live a useful and a happy life all the same. My ambition is to make you happy, not by shielding you from all that worries me—that would be the most effective way of grieving you—but by making you a sharer in joy and sorrow, pleasure and pain, in shade and sunshine."

At times he seemed to be nervous and slightly awkward in his unaccustomed role as lover. In a letter to Alice written while returning to Winnipeg after his proposal was finally accepted he described an odd sensation he felt in his bosom—"was it love or indigestion?" he asked. In a letter written on 10 June of 1889 he continued his theme of light-hearted self-abasement, this time with regard to his lack of stature as a man of fashion. He was not a dandy. "I have a genius," he wrote, "for spoiling clothes. I have often regretted my untidiness in matters of dress, but it seems to be born and bred in me. My barber gives me a lecture about once a week on my failure to slick up my hair; but that is a hopeless task for my hair defies all constituted authority. Where the curls have gone I cannot say. I never noticed their departure until Annette spoke of it when I went east and it now appears that you too noticed it. But they have certainly gone now and I have only got the ordinary shock of wiry red hair."

Alice, for her part, was not always able to manage a letter a day, but the letters from her kept coming. She joined in the literary discussions and they were pleased to discover that they liked many of the same authors and poets. She took an interest in his health, which at that time was not robust, and urged him to eat sensibly and get more sleep, sometimes pretending to be a nag on the subject. She filled him in on the Ottawa gossip, such as it was, and responded to his news from Winnipeg. Their letters became a conversation, back and forth across the miles of lake and forest that separated them. Sometimes the tone of the letters was serious, at other times a strong note of teasing levity crept in. They were learning to enjoy each other.

Jack haunted the post office at the Winnipeg railway station. He was there whenever a train came in from the East and was dashed when there was not a letter from Alice in the bag. The year that must pass before their wedding day arrived stretched before them like a cold wilderness.

MISSING HER/MISSING HIM

The shy couple had decided to keep their engagement a secret for a bit, but the news was soon out. One of the first to know about it was the bride-to-be's sister, Annette, as Alice reported in a letter to the prospective groom: "Annette walked part of the way home with me. One summer day nearly six years ago we were walking in Montreal and she told me of her engagement to Allan. It was a complete surprise to me and I never quite forgave her for telling me in the street where of course I could give no expression to my feelings. Now I thought is a splendid chance for revenge so I told her my happy secret. But, strange to relate, she was not at all surprised. She said too that when she first became acquainted with you she made up her mind that we were exactly suited for each other if we would only discover that fact for ourselves." A week or two later newspapers in Ottawa and Winnipeg were "scooped" when Jack's friends placed an announcement of the forthcoming wedding in the *Toronto World*.

Being away from Alice was a torment, but Jack found that keeping busy helped. "I am going on steadily with the work that comes to my hand and doing it earnestly and conscientiously," he told Alice in a letter. "Perhaps time will bring me added wealth and honours. I hope so, for I am becoming more ambitious than I was in the olden days." He was afflicted with the megrims, "but I went to work and soon my spirits had reached their wanted calm. A busy man I find is usually happy; therefore I propose to be a busy man."

There was no shortage of opportunities to be busy. He had taken on the duties of city editor and found it a challenge, as he would report to Alice: "I believe, after a good many years in newspaper work [six!], that the city editor has the most wearisome task on a newspaper. A night editor sits at his desk and his work comes to him. But a city editor's work is like a woman's— it is never done. He has miles of crowded city to look after and how to do it is a problem which has to be solved anew daily. It keeps one from rusting. If he does not keep right up to the mark the troublesome contemporary [opposition paper] gets the start of him in some important matters and then he feels how vain a thing is life. Still, I like the work; it brings me into constant contact with humanity, I see the light and shade of life. For studying character it is probably a unique position. I have learned to despise a good many men who hold their heads high in Winnipeg from what I have seen of them. Fancy a minister of the Gospel writing the most fulsome praise of his own sermon and sending it in for publication. That is by no means an infrequent occurrence. Then there is the man who tries to get items put in reflecting on somebody whom he doesn't like. I have become so hardened in course of time that I have no hesitation in snubbing men who come in with cheeky requests no matter who they are."

Newspapering had its ups and downs, however. "What an uneven life we newspapermen have," he told Alice. "Last week we were rushed to death and today we are all in despair as to what we will fill our paper with."

The life of a newsman could be full of unusual events. Later in the year he would describe a great buffalo roundup out on the prairie near Stony Mountain Penitentiary: "I had a big time yesterday, did not get home until late at night thoroughly chilled by a sixteen mile drive across the prairie in the face of a bitter wind. I went out there to watch some cowboys lasso and hobble some wild buffalo who have been sold to an American gentleman. They had a lovely time. I was one of a queer group of spectators who looked on at the fun from a safe stand-point. Let me see: there were in the little crowd of onlookers Miss Bedson, one of the daughters of the warden of the penitentiary, her brother, a guard with a rifle, two convicts and a lunatic—the last three under the charge of the guard—and your young man."

Jack's interest in domesticated buffalo had developed earlier in 1889 when his freelance article in *The Popular Science Monthly* on the subject had elicited a fan letter from Erastus Wiman, the notorious Canadian-born New York capitalist and advocate of a Canada-U.S. commercial union. Wiman, in his letter, urged Jack to keep the public informed on "this singular and interesting development," which may explain the young journalist's presence at Stony Mountain on that cold and windy day. There is no evidence that a follow-up article was written or that Jack responded to Wiman's invitation to meet in New York or Winnipeg to discuss buffalo and, possibly, free trade. Nevertheless, he was sufficiently impressed with Wiman's letter to save it all his life.

In another letter Jack dazzled—and possibly shocked— his bride-to-be with an account of a descent into the notorious Winnipeg underworld, described by some pious Eastern clergymen as Canada's closest equivalent of Sodom and Gomorrah. She would have been comforted, no doubt, by the fact that he was accompanied by a policeman: "The Chief of Police and I started out early in the afternoon to find a man. He was a hard citizen, a jailbird and a vagrant, but, by the whirligigs of fortune, he was in a position to give information which both the chief and I wanted to get. What a chase we had—through all the byways, alley ways, dives and taverns in the town until I felt positively ashamed of being in such localities. We found him, although it took until late in the night and although I did not get exactly what I wanted yet I got sufficient to get a scoop on our loathsome contemporary, and that rewarded me.

"Then just about midnight there was a rumour that a murder had been committed on the outskirts of the city and that kept me up for a couple of additional hours. It is a rum life we lead. We rub shoulders with all classes of society, see much that is noble and the reverse in human nature and yet I would not change it for any other business in the world, for I don't think I could be happy at anything else. So sweetheart you will have to resign yourself to the horrible fate of being all your life the partner in misfortune of a newspaper scribbler." With the passage of time, Alice would become accustomed to the vagaries of a scribbler's life and as she grew older she would become a keen fan of the detective novel and the murder mystery.

Freelance work was also keeping Jack busy, as it would for years to come. "I am working hard these days," he told Alice, "but there is this satisfaction in that my extra work is for Chicago and New York papers and that it will bring in a good many additional dollars which I will carefully put away for the proverbial rainy day." He was also writing for the *Toronto Globe* and contributing to a new Winnipeg gossip sheet, *Town Talk*, which was courting him as a possible editor. "I won't take the editorship of the paper," he assured Alice. "The most I'll do will be to write a couple of pages of matter for it weekly. I will look after the Athletic Department and will write them a weekly gossipy screed. I will have time for nothing else." He was becoming a journalist who could turn his hand to anything, from politics to sports and the gossip column.

Freelance work did not always bring quick returns, however, as he reported in a letter to Alice: "The *Chicago Times* owes me a couple of hundred dollars. I have been trying to convince them that I can be trusted with that amount, but as yet without success. If I get it out of them I will send half of it home. I will not miss it much and it may mean to them the difference between comfort and discomfort." Trouble at home was, unhappily, a fairly regular

occurrence as he confided to Alice in a letter written early in 1890:
"I got a letter from Father last night. I always know what that
means. He always lets the women folk do the correspondence excepting when he gets into a hole financially and swoops down on
me for help. This has been going on for ten years past and I have
always been able to help him, and I have always done it willingly.
The old gentleman has had a pretty hard row to hoe and although
had I chosen to be selfish I would probably be worth thousands
where I have hundreds yet I would rather have the knowledge
that I had lifted a few burdens from the shoulders of the old folks
than to have a fat bank balance—and so would you, I know. He
is gradually getting on his feet and last year was an unfortunate
one for Manitoba farmers and the old gentleman preferred coming to me instead of to someone who would charge him twenty-
five per-cent. I hope these financial troubles don't bore you, but I
have had to do for many years a good deal of the thinking, financ-
ing and worrying for the entire family, but I have my satisfaction
when I know that they are gradually bettering their condition. I
know that had I not been hampered I would now, comparatively
speaking, be well off in a material sense, but in another sense I
am rich—first in your love, affection and trust, secondly in the affection of my family. There is plenty of time remaining to retrieve
my material fortunes."

He was saving money by sharing digs, but found it not to
his liking. He had enjoyed sharing an apartment in Montreal because he had his own room. In a Winnipeg boarding house you
had to share a single room and that led to annoyance and fric-
tion. "I don't like Mr. Dodge as a room-mate," he complained in
a letter to Alice. "We don't suit one another exactly. Sometimes I
feel that his very presence is an irritant. I don't suppose there is
any sense in my dislike of him because he has many good qualities, but 'I do not like thee, Dr. Fell....' I have never tried rooming
with persons on an extensive scale. I usually prefer to be alone.

My first adventure of this sort was with Mr. Scott on O'Connor Street in Ottawa, just around the corner from your Maria Street house. He was altogether too irregular in his hours and snored too much for me and we dissolved partnership. I for about five months the winter after I came to Winnipeg roomed with a young man named Dawson Stephens—a fine young fellow. Then came my old friend Turner and then Dodge."

Alice began to feel that he was working too hard and she feared for his health. Jack attempted to calm her: "Not a week passes without someone on the FP being absent through illness, but with the exception of my famous attack of measles I have never missed a day at the office." He was willing to admit, however, that he was deficient in some respects. "I was quite humiliated the other day," he confessed, "to find that the junior reporter on the paper, several years my junior and a couple of inches shorter, was actually about 16 pounds heavier than I was. I would like to get some flesh on my bones, but I never knew a Dafoe yet who did not look like a telegraph pole and I will be no exception to the general rule. The sanguine temperament is not conducive to embonpoint. We will be an odd looking couple, you petite and neat and I tall and scraggy."

Alice herself was a bit worried about their "odd couple" problem. She was worried about meeting his kinfolk and was afraid that she was about to marry into a family of giants. "When I think of your family," she wrote, " I wish I were a few inches taller. It is only the first shock of surprise when they see me that I am afraid of. Be sure you prepare them."

Jack had consulted a doctor about shooting pains in his arms and chest, the doctor diagnosing that Victorian medical standby a "nervous disorder" and prescribing a tonic. Jack advised Alice to remain calm. "I expect to be one of the oldest inhabitants about the middle of the next century who will occasionally give the million inhabitants who will then reside in Winnipeg pointers about the weather and other topics on which I will pose as an authority. Altogether, I think the Dafoes can compete with the Parmelees in the longevity line; the only way they can get us under the ground is to kill us."

Nevertheless, Alice worried about him. "Take good care of yourself, dear," she wrote. "Do you think working 14 hours a day is the way to keep well?" Later in the year she would renew the attack with a bit of cheerful nagging: "Do you think you will be obeying my commands and taking a complete rest when you are writing an article for the Christmas *Globe*?" It was no use, he loved being busy. He would work hard all his life.

He sent Alice an engagement ring by mail, regretting that he would not be at hand to put it on her finger and be awarded the kiss that usually follows the presentation of such a gift. Her letter of thanks, which arrived three days later, almost compensated for the loss: "My Dear Jack," she wrote," I am sitting Turkish fashion near the window in my room in the attic whither I have fled from the madding crowd. I am surrounded with treasures. On my finger is the most beautiful ring I ever saw—my dear boy I wish you were here to put it on for me, quite as much as you can wish it—beside me are your last letters, your pictures are on the wall above me. My inkstand is on a box which contains some roses. That little ring means a great deal to me. My irrepressible small brother Wilf says I grin every time I look at it."

To help pass the time in far-off Winnipeg, Jack was beginning to write short stories and wrestling once again with the old question about whether his future lay with journalism or with literature. His old Montreal friend George Iles, now connected to the New York publishing house of Appleton and Co, kept writing to tell him that he was wasting his time in the Canadian North-West. Even his chief at the *Free Press*, W.F. Luxton, suggested that he might have a bright future as a man of letters. Jack himself was not so certain. Even Alice wondered if he was possibly intended for better things. Several months before their wedding Jack responded to her concerns: "So you want me to discuss seriously my reasons for keeping out of literature and devoting myself to journalism. Really, I very much doubt whether I possess talent enough to ever amount to much in literature and it is a bad profession to go into unless one can reach the top or near it. Another reason: I doubt whether I know enough for such a career. I left school when I was fourteen and though I have picked up a lot of information since then there are sad gaps in my knowledge. On the other hand, I like journalism and in that profession I have confidence. I am not very far from the top in it now and I feel I can climb the remaining distance. Of course a large proportion of a newspaperman's work is drudgery and routine, but on the whole it is a fascinating life and suits my nature. There is a current saying in the newspaper world that if a man gets a drop of newspaper ink in his veins it never gets out as long as he lives. I think I can make a success of journalism, whereas I fear I would be a failure at literature. If I wanted to live by my pen pure and simple I would have to go across the line and I don't care about turning Yankee just yet. No, I'll keep pegging away at the humdrum life of a journalist."

He was, however, still not quite certain what branch of journalism he would eventually concentrate on. He had spent much of his career so far covering politics and had been disconcerted by the generally low level of Canadian political activity. In a letter to Alice he described the Manitoba legislature as "a regular Kilkenny cat fight." Still, he was torn. "I propose devoting myself more to the literary than to the political side of journalism," he wrote, "although under certain circumstances I think I could throw myself heart and soul into a political struggle—such, for instance, as a fight for Canadian independence." His role in the battle, however, would be conducted with a pen behind the scenes, not on the political platform. The life of a politician was not for him, he declared in a letter to Alice. "If I should ever in the future be so insane as to show any inclination to go into politics," he wrote, "I hope you will set down your foot with a dull, sickening thud that will be heard for several townships around. Very few men can go through a political baptism and come out as good as they went in—it makes liars and time-servers of most men." Years later, another harsh criticism of political life would be attributed to him: "There are only two kinds of government, the scarcely tolerable and the absolutely unbearable."

Meanwhile, he had been reading Ibsen's *A Doll's House* and it struck a chord in him. "I have always believed," he told Alice, "that women and men should stand equal in all things." His ideal wife, he wrote, should be "a companion, advisor, friend; a partner indeed in all the varying labours and pleasures of life. I venture to say," he added, "that you will never be a doll wife to me—but always a woman demanding respect and honour and love for qualities of heart and head." They would remain together for over half a century and to the end she would remain his closest companion, advisor and friend.

Alice herself had her own view of Ibsen's play: "Being a woman," she wrote, "I shall probably find it even more interesting than you did. The subject is one that I have thought a good deal about and suffered over. Suffered—that may sound extravagant but it is not an exaggeration. There are so many men who have what Ibsen has called the oriental idea and I can believe that there never was a wife of such a man who did not in her heart passionately protest against it."

Music was an important part of Alice's life in Ottawa. She and her sisters attended concerts and musical evenings in private homes and Alice was learning to play the piano. She enjoyed her lessons, but complained to Jack that she had been asked to perform "The Dying Poet" by Louis Moreau Gottschalk, a work she found to be lugubrious and boring. Her father, listening to her working on the piece, suggested that the poet was obviously dying of a rattlesnake bite. Jack was also discovering music in Winnipeg, although he was aware that his musical knowledge was inferior to that of his bride-to-be. "As for me," he wrote, "I have a soul, but no ear, for music. That is, I like music of pretty nearly every kind. I have even stood at a street corner and listened to a hurdy-gurdy droning out Only a Pansy Blossom, Sweet Violets, Molly Darling and other melodies of that class and have been rather sorry when the grinder gathered up his pennies and moved off. I went to a concert by the Mendelssohn Quintet about a month ago. I didn't know what they were playing and didn't want to. It pleased me and rested me and I was satisfied." His favourite song was "Annie Laurie."

It had been a cold spring, especially at night, with constant north winds. "Everyone," Jack reported on 28 May 1889, "has colds." On 30 June the temperature in Winnipeg stood at 100 and Jack, sweltering at the *Free Press* office, took pen in hand to describe for Alice the disconcerting extremes of weather she would encounter when she came to live with him in the prairie city: "it is a terribly warm day and when it is warm in Manitoba there is no doubt about it. This is an emphatic climate. When it is cold you fancy that the North Pole is on the next lot; when it is hot you come to believe that the geographers have run the equator in the wrong place. When the wind blows everything goes. And when the weather lays itself out to give us a perfect day, I don't think any climate in the world can do better. We have many perfect days, particularly in the autumn. Just at present we are in for the hot spell and accordingly we are broiling under a merciless sun and a cloudless sky. However, with some exceptions, the nights are cool and there is always a pleasant breeze from the prairie making life endurable."

On warm summer evenings there was plenty to do in the prairie city. Being manager of the lacrosse team kept him busy—sometimes too busy—and he kept planning to resign. A team outing to Portage la Prairie in July to play a local team at a Sunday school picnic took up an entire day. To Jack's annoyance, the game was rained out. Rowing was a new pleasure and he loved to take his boat on the Red River to the Forks and along the Assiniboine to the St. James rapids, then "lie down in the bottom of my boat and let the swift current sweep me down until I found myself again upon the broad bosom of the Red. Many a dream I dreamed lying in the old boat." Not surprisingly, boating accidents were not uncommon on the river, although Jack's luck held. Less fortunate was a party of local Americans, including the popular Rev. F.B. Duval and James Wickes Taylor, the U.S. consul. Their boat, the *Antelope*, was stuck on a rock in the middle of the river for much of the afternoon during July 4 celebrations while the band played the "Star Spangled Banner." Rescue was slow in coming, Jack reported in a letter to Alice. "W.H. Thompson and I pulled up to the scene of the disaster in one of the racing boats of the Winnipeg Rowing Club and rescued another member of the club who was discovered showing signs of distress on the deck."

There were many picnics and sports days during the warm summer months. At one picnic Jack served as a judge of sports competitions, standing in the sun for hours. He went home with a raging headache. At another outing he beat all the other editors in town in a foot race.

There were political issues, as well, to help warm the air in Manitoba that summer. At a meeting in Portage la Prairie in August at which Jack was present the Francophobe politician D'Alton McCarthy, supported by a Manitoba cabinet minister, Joe Martin, attacked the school and language rights enjoyed by Franco-Manitobans and Roman Catholics under the Manitoba Act of 1870. The "Manitoba School Question," beginning as a local grass fire, would be a central issue in Canadian politics for the next decade and beyond. Later in the year he would tell Alice that "I have an article in the last *Toronto Week* on the Manitoba School Question. Mr. Luxton was highly complimentary about it today and said he was going to reproduce it in the *Free Press.*" During the next decade Jack would have much more to say about the matter.

By the end of August Jack had begun to feel that life without Alice was unending torture in spite of the pleasant flow of letters between Winnipeg and Ottawa. In early September he took some holidays and made his way East via Port Arthur and Lake Superior. He was sick on the steamer, but suffering faded away as the train pulled into Ottawa and he saw Alice and her parents standing on the platform. In the days that followed there were walks and picnics and lively evenings of whist and music in the Parmelee's parlour. There were, presumably, games of cribbage with Mr. Parmelee, although Jack later complained to Alice that he had not been introduced to her father's friend Wing On, a Chinese gentleman who came to Slater Street for English lessons. "Evidently," he wrote, "your sister Julia has the inside track in the affections of your father's chum Wing On. Extend her my congratulations on her conquest of the Flowery Kingdom. I have never met the redoubtable Wing On but I have no doubt he is a very interesting individual."

All too soon the holiday was over and Jack set out on his homeward journey via Toronto, where he took in the Exhibition and visited some old newspaper friends at the offices of the Empire. But he found Toronto "uninteresting after Ottawa" and cut his visit short, moving on to the port at Collingwood where he met many Winnipeggers boarding the *Alberta* for the journey west. In a letter to Alice posted at Port Arthur he provided a lively account of the rigours of the lake passage: "Got here at midnight last night, fifteen hours behind time after one of the stormiest voyages the *Alberta* ever made or will ever make. She tossed about like a cork. I was lying on my berth. One moment I was standing on my head and the next on my feet so great was the roll and with every pitch there was a crash of crockery in the kitchen. I stood the storm very much better than expected." As the ship entered Thunder Bay he was able to eat some crackers and cheese while a number of Winnipeggers who had laughed at his seasickness on the outward voyage moaned in agony.

He arrived back in Winnipeg in time to witness the visit of "his nibs" the Governor-General, Lord Stanley, and his lady. The vice-regal couple was accorded a torch-light parade through the streets of the city and a stuffy reception or "drawing room" in the hall of the legislature. "My dislike of a dress suit," he reported to Alice, "does not mark me out as an exception in Winnipeg." The drawing room "was in the hands of those who consider themselves the bon ton of the city and the ukase went forth that all who desired to enjoy the great honour of a handshake with Lord Stanley must appear in full dress! The plebeians dressed in common attire could look on from the gallery. The result was that about seventy five individuals appeared on the floor of the chamber and were presented while three or four hundred of the best citizens of Winnipeg attired in pretty fair tweed suits looked on at the proceedings. His Excellency sizing things up announced that he would like to meet all those in the building and so the plebs filed down from the gallery and the reception was saved from being a disastrous fizzle. It was a great victory for the unconventionalism of the democratic West. I don't go much for shows of this sort. In all the sessions I was in Ottawa I never attended any of the drawing rooms. I never could see the utility of them. And one of the reasons why I took so strong a liking to the Parmelee family as a whole and you in particular was because you did not seem to take much stock of them either."

As the year wore on he continued to be a regular visitor to the theatres of Winnipeg. One theatre, he would later report, stood about 50 yards from the front door of the house in which he and Alice would live after the wedding. He was sorry, however, that the touring and stock companies—British, Canadian and American—were not of the first rank. One regular visitor to Winnipeg at this time was the American Thomas Keene, later described as being "a large, florid man, old fashioned in his acting, being most popular in the smaller and less sophisticated cities." In early 1890 Jack saw Keene in *Richard III*, in *Richelieu*, in *Hamlet* and in *The Merchant of Venice*. At another theatre in the same month the versatile Mrs. Prescott, described by Jack as "about the best actress in Shakespeare's plays that I have ever seen," was appearing as Perdita in *A Winter's Tale* and, oddly, as Iago in *Othello*. "It has always been a very keen regret to me," he told Alice, "that I missed seeing Henry Irving and Ellen Terry when they were in Montreal in 1884. I went home on a visit the week before they arrived. It will be a long time before Winnipeg is a place of sufficient importance to draw first class actors here." In fact, top companies would be visiting the city regularly before too many years had passed. In the meantime Jack made the best of what was available, attending performances given by visiting troupes and by the local stock company that featured a number of former members of the recently disbanded Eugene A. McDowell troupe, an all-Canadian company from Montreal. In a letter to Alice, written after he had attended a matinee performance of The *School for Scandal*, Jack indulged in a bit of drama criticism: "It was played by a stock company which grinds out two dramas per week at the city theatre and, accordingly, it was not done full justice to, yet I enjoyed it. Strange to say, it was the first time I had ever seen the comedy played by any company. Mrs. McDowell—Fanny Reeves—did you ever see her?—played Lady Teazle. She is a very charming actress and, I am told, a very refined and cultured lady. She is married to an arrogant, conceited, bumptious, jack'anapes of a fellow whom I despise as an actor and as a man." His reasons for disliking E.A. McDowell are not mentioned. Perhaps he had attempted an interview with the actor while on the "hotel beat" in Montreal. News of McDowell's status as an object of scorn may have been conveyed to him by his close friend Charles Wesley Handscomb, city editor of the rival *Manitoban*, future drama editor of the *Free Press* and the author of a melodrama, *The Big Boom*, produced in Winnipeg in 1886 by the McDowell troupe. Handscomb, it appears, had been taken up by McDowell, presumably puffed up as the great hope of Canadian theatre, then ignominiously dumped, a Canadian theatrical tradition that endures to this day.

On Sunday nights as Jack rested after dinner in the boarding house on Notre Dame, there was always his leather-bound copy of *John Gilbert's Shakespeare*, with Gilbert's pen drawings of Falstaff and Romeo, Lear, Hamlet, Prospero and Portia, to dip into in the hour before sleep. It had entertained him since his school days, a boon companion in Combermere, Bark Lake, Arnprior, Montreal, Ottawa and now Winnipeg. He would keep it close at hand all his days and it would endure as a family heirloom long after his departure. It sits, a battered and crumbling hulk, on his old writing desk beside the computer as these words are written more than a century after that hot Manitoba summer of 1889.

WINTER DREAMS

Cold rain was falling when Jack got back from the East, but soon the long, golden western autumn was spreading itself over the prairie. Then there were warm, dry Saturday afternoons for lacrosse and football games or boat trips along the river as the smoke from burning stubble drifted by on the breeze. The open country was near at hand and Jack walked for miles through the long grass, leaving the small city far behind. The clumps of oaks, Manitoba maples and cottonwoods along the roads and the river and the poplars rising up in little islands in the great oceanic expanse of open plain were red, yellow and dark gold in the bright sunshine. At night, as he walked back to the boarding house or lay in his bed waiting for sleep he could hear the shouting of geese as they passed far above the city, the lakes and the marsh already miles behind them as they rushed south. "September," he had told Alice, "is the finest month of the year, the days bright and sun-shiney, but not too warm, the nights clear and cool." Autumn would always be his favourite season in Manitoba.

He was looking forward to going East again in the new year to cover the Parliamentary session and to spend time with Alice and her family at 128 Slater Street. In the meantime he was getting back into the busy routine of daily newspapering at the *Free Press*. In a letter to Alice he outlined a "specimen day:" "I got up at noon. By one I was at the office where I stayed until six. By eight o'clock I was again at my desk which I did not leave until a few minutes ago when I blew out the lamps and headed for home just at three o'clock. It isn't as bad as it once was when we never got the paper up until four and sometimes later. Those were hard days. I don't yearn for their return. We are publishing a pretty nice paper just at present. I must send you a copy now and then for I don't suppose you ever see it in Ottawa. It is a good newspaper for a smaller town than Ottawa to turn out." It was a hectic life, but he loved it. He would work long hours all his days. In a letter written to Alice in October he informed her that "I am really getting back to my old industrious habits when I could work from early morning until late at night with scarcely a flagging of energy. Work never injured me, but worry knocks me out in no time."

As Jack rattled on in letter after letter about how busy he was, Alice, fretting in Ottawa, began, once again, to worry about his health. He was freelancing for papers in New York, Chicago and Toronto. On top of his daily chores in the *Free Press* newsroom he was working on a big Christmas supplement for the paper and writing the weekly sports and gossip columns for *Town Talk*. Early in November the bride-to-be probably had mixed feelings when Jack told her of some more work that was likely coming his way: "Have you seen the prospectus of the new national magazine to be established in Toronto in early February? I saw one today and was somewhat surprised to see my name among the list of persons who are expected to contribute. It was the first I had heard of the matter. I did not object to seeing my name there for all these little things help a newspaperman. As in every calling, a reputation is half the battle and one mediocre signed article in a magazine does a man more good in the profession than a year of good anonymous work."

The big Christmas supplement was a sore point, as he reported to Alice in a November letter: "I am deep in the mysteries of the Christmas edition. Mr. Payne and I over a month ago began work on it, but Mr. Luxton vetoed it—said we would not have a special edition this year as it was too much trouble. He said that last year and the year before, but Payne and I argued the point with him and secured the day. But this year when he squelched us we got mad and let the matter slide. Why should we insist on bringing a great deal of extra trouble and worry on our shoulders particularly when our superior was not desirous that the work should be undertaken? And now after a precious month of time has been wasted the fiat has gone forth that there is to be a special edition at Christmas, and Mr. Payne and I have got on our thinking caps. The extra work will fall almost exclusively on Payne and I and it really is a very difficult task because we have very little scope to secure outside aid. Last year I guess I wrote fully half of the original material myself. For the past two years I have furnished an original story based on the good old Christmas plan and I have undergone considerable chaffing on that account. I don't think I'll write one this year. I fear the reading public would say 'Rats!' if they saw my name in type below another sentimental yarn." Just the same, space had to be filled and Jack soon found himself dishing out purple prose designed to rattle the heart strings—and hating every minute of it. The life of a journalist could be a nightmare at times.

Busy as he was, Jack was also finding time to get out of doors almost every day for a vigorous tramp to look at a sunset or explore one of the many creeks that fed the Red and Assiniboine rivers. The long, lazy autumn dragged on and then, quite suddenly, as it does in Manitoba, winter blew in. In his letter to Alice for 25 November 1889 he told of a blizzard in the offing: "I think we are on the eve of a big snow storm. I hope so. My snowshoes over in the corner look ready for business and I would like a brisk six-mile walk across country under a starry sky." He was not to be disappointed. A day later he was writing: "We have a rare old snow storm raging today. There is something in a snow storm that always delights. I like to go out in it, to feel the snow beat against my face. I am going to go for a walk after I finish this letter." The snow had arrived to stay. A week or two later he was describing a moonlit tramp of the snowshoe club across the prairie, adding, to calm Alice's fears about his health, the comforting news that "I find a brisk five-mile run across the prairie a healing experience."

In Winnipeg there were also debates, controversies and shouting matches to get pulled into, especially when religion was the topic. In one letter Jack reported on one of them: "Spent an hour or so in heated controversy with a couple of ultra-Protestants who believed that Catholics can be made Protestant by an Act of Parliament."

Work on the Christmas supplement was proceeding and the arrival of snow had been inspirational, up to a point: "Another fall of snow last night has given us sleighing and the jingle of bells from the street reaches me as I write. As today is municipal election day there are a great many rigs on the street and it has given the city quite a gay appearance." The committee of the snowshoes club was also inspired by the arrival of the snow and was thinking of starting a "ladies' night." Jack did not think it would work: "It's too cold a country for spooning and snowshoeing at the same time—and that's what ladies' night means."

At home in Ottawa Alice watched the arrival of the Eastern winter and walked every morning to her job at the sugar testing lab on Parliament Hill. In the evening after dinner she had to write fast in order to get her letter to Jack finished so that her young brothers could drop it off at the post office on their way to hockey practice. She knew that Jack would be waiting at the station in Winnipeg when the mailbag from Ottawa arrived. Social obligations cut into her letter-writing time and invitations to parties and "card nights" kept coming in. She begged off one euchre party and was disappointed to learn that she had missed meeting the poet Archibald Lampman and his wife. One friend of the family organized a special dinner party so that Alice's friends could get a last look at her before she was carried off to the Wild West, never to be seen again. Meanwhile, she was learning to cook and asked Jack to get recipes for his favourite meals from his mother. After their marriage, as soon as they could afford it, they hired a cook.

And so their letters went back and forth as winter closed over them. In Ottawa Alice's social life continued to hum along. There were concerts to attend, evenings at home with the usual crowd of visitors, church, dinner parties, the winter carnival on the Rideau rink—which she attended with her mother—and visits with friends and relations in the Townships. For Jack, alone in the West, there was time to dream as he walked along the rivers on cold Sunday afternoons or through the empty streets at three in the morning after putting the paper "to bed." In a letter to Alice later in the winter he wrote that "I am feeling these days what a glorious thing it is to be young and strong with the world before me and in the knowledge that my 'heart's delight' will share my journey with me."

He had much to think of. His journey, in a way, had only just begun, but he had already travelled far from the settlement at Combermere and the rough schoolhouse at Bark Lake. Whatever it was elsewhere, in Canada the nineteenth century was a time of opportunity and widening horizons for those born poor but willing to dream and strive and Jack, like a character from one of the uplifting books by Horatio Alger, was making the most of it. The son of a semi-literate farmer and lumberjack and a mother who had obtained much of her meagre education at Sunday school had stepped out of the backwoods at seventeen and landed a job on a rising Montreal newspaper, becoming, in a few months, that newspaper's correspondent in the national capital. He had become acquainted with a future prime minister and knew important men in Ottawa, Montreal and Quebec City. Then he had served—briefly and unsuccessfully to be sure, but no hard lesson is ever wasted—as editor of a new daily paper. Now, at 23, he

was engaged to the well-educated daughter of a senior civil servant, he was writing for newspapers and magazines all over North
America and everyone who knew him was certain that he would
go far. Some—especially his parents—may have been amazed at
his rapid progress. His old grandfather, John Elcome the Kentish
Chartist, dead since Jack was seven, might not have been surprised
had he known and it seems likely that Jack himself was already
well aware that interesting adventures awaited him on the road
ahead. He had felt the power within himself, but he was aware,
nevertheless, that he had much to learn. His was to be a journalist's education, based on wide reading, extensive personal experience and contact with many minds. Accomplishing it would
consume a lifetime.

Later he would be described as a "self-made man," but even
in his early twenties, when all the world seemed spread out before
him, he was aware that no man is ever "self-made." The world
would be his university. He was a true child of the nineteenth
century, a product of the "Age of Improvement," a Victorian who
struggled with all the doubts and uncertainties of the times. The
Victorian high noon had given way to the shadows of approaching evening and Jack, for all his youthful enthusiasm, was aware,
as well, that the world was not as stable as had been supposed
and that the new century, for which his generation would be responsible, promised to be a time of danger and perplexing change.

As the winter of 1889 advanced he continued his studies in
the cold boarding house bedroom, propped up in a chair under a
blanket or tucked under the covers in bed, the oil lamp casting its
pale light though the shadows. In a letter to Alice in mid-October
he had written "I am making a start at Goethe's works and will
try and get through them all by the New Year. I often wonder
how men who never read get along in the newspaper business
as many of them do. They must have greater natural advantages
than we who have daily to be restoring the waste of our minds.

I usually get an hour or so of reading when I go home at night while my room-mate is calmly sleeping away and much ground can be covered in an hour a day spent judiciously. I hope in the future to be doing a great deal of reading with you. I almost despair of ever being more than a fair to middling hack writer, but if I should sometime get into the higher worlds of literature, I expect it will be very largely your encouragement and assistance that will place me there."

He was reading Herbert Spencer and Henry George, the novels of Sir Walter Scott, George Meredith, R.D. Blackmore, William Makepeace Thackeray and Charles Dickens, magazines such as *The Century*, *North American Review*, *The Atlantic*, *Harper's* and *Scribner's*. He read Walt Whitman's *Specimen Days* and recommended it to Alice. A year earlier he had discovered a copy of the Routledge's Popular Library edition of Emerson's essays in a Winnipeg book shop and he had trudged through it, from the essay on history to the essays on the conduct of life and self-reliance, then on, through six hundred pages of small type set in two columns, to the letter on Transcendentalism, underlining choice passages as he went. He read John Stuart Mill's essay "On Liberty" and Walter Bagehot on the English constitution and discovered the tales of Guy de Maupassant and the poetry of Robert Browning. Tennyson remained a favourite. At Mortimore's book shop on Main Street he found Professor Arthur Galton's popular anthology of English prose in *The Camelot Series*. It was the sort of handy volume that he loved to slip into his pocket to read on the train, on the boat or on a country walk, a kind of portable university that served as his first introduction to works such as Sir Thomas Browne's *Religio Medici*, Robert Burton's *Anatomy of Melancholy*, Jonathon Swift's *The Battle of the Books*, Thomas Mallory's *Morte D'Arthur* and Milton's *Areopagitica*. The pile of books beside his bed grew higher and he reached into it according to his mood, selecting poetry, political economy, history, a play or a novel. He kept a scrapbook of articles, drawings and poems that he cut out of literary reviews and he began a lifelong habit of clipping items from newspapers and squirreling them away in box files and between the pages of books. He collected quotations in a Commonplace book. He bought a glass-fronted bookcase with a lock, filled it with books, locked it and promptly lost the key. The novels and stories of Thomas Hardy had a special appeal for him. Their depictions of rural life and the struggles of those determined to rise in the world reminded him of his own struggle for self-improvement and advancement. Throughout his life he would return again and again to Hardy's novels, short stories and poems. One Hardy novel, especially, spoke strongly to him, as he reminded Alice in a letter written in December 1913: "I went home Saturday night about 8:30, got into the big chair at the library end of the sitting room and forgot myself in a book. The book I pulled out almost at random was *Jude the Obscure*. Not a very cheerful choice, but the tragedy was old to me while the treatment was, as always, new. Isn't it just about the greatest book Hardy ever wrote?"

His social life was not extensive. There is no evidence to suggest that he was a regular churchgoer, Sundays usually being reserved for sleeping late, reading and outdoor exercise. Not being a drinking man, he avoided the bars and saloons, missing out on some of the companionship that newsmen have traditionally found in such places. He was a member of the Press Club and attended its dinner meetings, but confessed in a letter to Alice that he had made few new friendships among fellow journalists, among the exceptions being Charles Wesley Handscomb who shared, apart from his middle name, his interest in theatre, and his *Free Press* colleague Walter Payne. He occasionally visited a married couple, the Days, for dinner and a game of cribbage, but he appears to have been, essentially, a lone wolf.

His family, austere in its Methodism and traditionally short of money, had never formerly set much store by Christmas. Taken as a whole," Jack admitted, "the Dafoes are undemonstrative and although there is between us a very firm bond of friendship and love, it is shown but little among the members of the family." In a letter mailed in late November he told Alice that he had not been home for Christmas since 1882. This year, however, Christmas in Killarney would be combined with his sister Edith's marriage to Charles Fowler and Jack would be there. He also intended to continue a custom of several years standing of showering his family with gifts. In a letter to Alice in early December he set out his plan: "The modus operandi of my bringing Christmas presents to the folks at home is very simple. Alex Taylor the stationer gets a large packing case ready for me and then I put all sorts of odds and ends into it. Books of adventure for the boys, toys for the second generation of little girls, books for the grown people, stray copies of magazines and odds and ends of all sorts. Then I express it to Killarney and I have no doubt but what the opening of the box creates considerable excitement in the Dafoe cottage. Most of my presents are books, which are appreciated on the prairie in winter time—and pretty good books too. I have sent Wallace for the past six years the bound volumes of the *Boy's Own Paper* which always goes the rounds of the settlement. Last year I sent Ted the James Fenimore Cooper *Leatherstocking Tales* and he went wild over them. My brothers are all very fond of reading, which is a good sign. I think they will grow into good, intelligent men. Yes, I think I'll buy father a pipe. I have never given the old gentleman the slightest semblance of a present at Christmas and the only thing he ever gave me was a rare old hiding one Christmas Eve when I was a little shaver about four."

His parents, in fact, had grown less stern with the passing years and in time became valued members of their community in southwestern Manitoba, his mother often conducting prayer meetings in the Methodist hinterland before the arrival of a permanent minister in 1891. She was superintendant of the Methodist

Sunday school and, it is reported, a friend to everyone. The writer Lillian Beynon Thomas, who came to the Killarney area as a country school teacher in the late 1890s, remembered all her life the warmth of her welcome to the Dafoe farmhouse: "She invited me to her home and Saturday after Saturday I walked four miles across wild prairie just to visit with her for a little while." Another visitor described Jack's mother as "a saint." Jack, perhaps due to an overdose of earnest "old time" religion in childhood, usually went for a walk at prayer time when home on a visit. After his marriage to Alice he was, nominally, a sedate Anglican, but was seldom seen at church, except for weddings and funerals.

Jack's younger bothers were growing up. Wallace was sixteen and Jack's plan was to bring him to Winnipeg to finish high school after he and Alice set up their home in the city, Wallace occupying the spare bedroom. A career in journalism would follow. Ted, at fourteen, was "already a man," according to Jack, "the handsome man of the family, already planning his own farm." Poor Teddy would not live to see his dream come true. Typhoid fever would soon cut him down. Calvin was twelve and already interested in carpentry and building. It would be his life's work. Rance, at ten, had firm plans: "He said very emphatically," Jack reported, "that he was going to stay at home until he was seventeen and then he was going to come into Winnipeg and make me get him a job." When the time came Jack was to find himself powerless to resist Rance's ambition to be a newspaperman.

On his return from Killarney Jack found the *Free Press* in turmoil. Several staff members were off sick, including news editor Walter Payne, and several others, including the two sons of the editor, had departed for other careers. It was a mixed blessing. "I am getting my staff reorganized," Jack told Alice in a letter mailed in early January. "I have got rid of both the Luxton boys. They were not of much use I must confess. I have got George Ham on temporarily and am trying to fix it permanently. George is about the King Bee of North West newspapermen. He was city editor of the *Free Press* about ten or twelve years ago and has had quite a chequered career since then, full of ups and downs all of which have been borne with the good nature of the genuine Bohemian. There is a great deal to having good men about one and I have had enough of amateurs for a while to come."

All this meant, of course, that Jack would not be able to go to Ottawa for the Parliamentary session. Mr. Ham would go instead. "My judgment told me that my place is at my desk," Jack wrote. He was working as city editor, night editor and reporter, putting in long hours. To Alice's disappointment was added the upsetting news that a typhoid fever epidemic was sweeping Winnipeg and had already killed a member of the lacrosse team. Jack's nose had frozen during an evening tramp with the snowshoe club, being further damaged in a fall down the riverbank. On top of it all Jack would be working all hours at the *Free Press* and wearing himself out instead of enjoying the healthy winter weather in Ottawa and resting in the front parlour at 128 Slater Street. "Newsmen," Alice observed bitterly, "work themselves to death." Jack, for his part, was attempting to pull himself together, possibly the result of a New Year's resolution. In a letter to Alice mailed on 11 January 1890 he admitted the need for personal improvement: "I will have about two hours left before tea to attend to a lot of things that have been accumulating: Trivial things such as a visit to the barber shop, a call on a tailor and so forth, but very essential if I am to remain even half decent in appearance. My hair has gown until I look like the Wild Man of Borneo and I have gone for days without a shave. It is easy enough to see that my young woman does not live in Winnipeg. You will have to get some nice little curtain lectures ready on the evils of untidiness."

Meanwhile, winter dragged on. "We are having," Jack wrote in his letter for 17 January, "intensely cold weather here just at present—46 below zero this morning." There was a touch of spring in early February and then, as it does in Manitoba, winter returned in earnest. The worst blizzard in eight years struck on 9 February, just as Jack was absorbing the distressing news that the June wedding might have to be postponed. Mr. Parmelee, it had been revealed, was expected to accompany the Honourable Mackenzie Bowell on a trade mission to Australia. The journey would last six months. For a moment there was consternation in Winnipeg and Ottawa and then, in answer to many prayers, the trade mission was postponed to a later date.

As February advanced hundreds of curlers had descended on the city for a bonspiel, their arrival followed by the traditional "bonspiel thaw." In the Manitoba Legislature the government was pushing through a bill to abolish French as an official language. There were signs of things to come. In his letter for February 28 Jack reported that "I was in to my tailor the other day trying on my wedding coat and vest." In early May, a few weeks before it snowed for the last time that winter, Jack moved into a rented house at 85 Notre Dame and began to get it ready for the arrival of his bride—and his brother Wallace who would be moving in with them. Alice's views on the proposed house guest are not recorded.

It was clear to both of them, however, that great things were in the offing. Jack, in a letter to Alice in late December, had put it this way: "1889-1890! What years they will be to us!"

A MYSTERY AT MURDER GULCH: JACK INVESTIGATES

Information from the distant past often comes to light in strange and unexpected ways. The mystery story that follows begins innocently enough. While sorting out some nineteenth-century family correspondence, the author of this biography came across a letter that appeared to be in the wrong transfer case. The postmark on the envelope is "Ottawa Feb 8 1921" and the sepia three-cent stamp features the bearded profile of King George V. What is this letter doing in the file containing letters from the 1880s? What mystery is here?

It soon appears that there are several mysteries. Inside the 1921 envelope, which is addressed to "Mrs. J.W. Dafoe 509 Spence St. Winnipeg Manitoba" is a four-page, handwritten document with an interesting letterhead: "The Manitoba Free Press Coy., morning, evening and weekly, W.F. Luxton, Managing Director." We are suddenly back in the late nineteenth century in the rising city of Winnipeg.

One mystery is quickly cleared up. The writing on the document is in the youthful hand of Jack Dafoe, then city editor and reporter on Luxton's paper. The document at hand appears to have been written by him toward the end of 1889, not as a letter to Alice, but notes prepared for perusal by her father In his capacity as a federal government official. It describes the mysterious discovery by a survey party of scattered human remains in what is now southeastern Saskatchewan and which was then part of the North-West Territories, a region just beginning to attract large numbers of settlers.

The puzzle of the 1921 envelope and post mark is also swiftly solved. A note on the back of the 1889 document reads "Found this in couch today. Will it interest Jack any?" The note is signed "Jewel." That would be Alice's younger sister, Miss Julia Parmelee of Ottawa, who seems to have discovered the 1889 pages pushed down under the springs or horsehair cushions of a couch where they may have been lost 30 years before. Historic documents, as many historians have discovered, are where you find them. Jack was clearly interested in this vintage example of his reporting in the 1880s, putting the document in a safe place where it was discovered more than a century after it was written and a lifetime after it was fortuitously retrieved from Great-Aunt Julia's commodious couch in Ottawa.

The story seems to have come to public attention in the autumn of 1889 when members of the Canadian survey party sent back reports of the discovery of the human bones and abandoned carts. The *Free Press* duly reported the grisly find and before long various well-meaning Western old-timers were in touch with the paper to add "details" to the story. On October 9, for example, the paper reported that "in conversation with a reporter of the *Free Press* concerning the finding by a survey party of several skeletons, some broken carts and a pile of empty cartridge shells, Mr. Latouche Tupper said he felt almost certain that the fight took place in 1879 when a band of Mandrils or Gros Ventres came across from the United States side of the line and attacked a party of Stonies of Ocean Man's band. About fourteen, Mr. Tupper thinks, were killed in the fight. Only one scalp was taken by the Stonies, but they had seven rifles, the owners of which were killed, it is presumed. Among the killed were two of Ocean Man's brothers. Mr. A. McDonald of the HB Co., now of Qu'Appelle, and Donald Armit of the same company now stationed at Lake Manitoba, doubtless will remember the locality of the fight and other particulars."

Nowadays a reporter would simply pick up the telephone or activate the Blackberry or the laptop and contact messrs McDonald and Armit for further details. The reporter of 1886, likely Jack Dafoe himself, had clearly failed to reach the Hudson's Bay Company traders and hoped they would read the story in the paper at some point—or hear of it—and get in touch. They never did respond and are now beyond reach. Latouche Tupper was easy to find, being a well-known Winnipeg character of the day, famous during the land boom earlier in the decade when he was said to have cleared ten to fifteen thousand dollars a day on land speculation—at least "in his own mind," according to George Ham who remembered Tupper when he was writing his memoirs in the 1920s.

Although McDonald and Armit were not heard from, a correspondent at Prince Albert, C.R. Stovel, wrote to confirm Tupper's recollection: "Chief Ocean Man's band and another band under Chief Pheasant Rhump (both Stonies) came to reside on their reserves at Moose Mountain shortly after this occurrence and brought with them the bodies of those killed which were buried in the Stony fashion, consisting of being wrapped in their blankets and placed on a platform supported by poles and raised to a height of five feet from the ground. The number of the buried was, I think, twelve or fourteen."

All very well, but what about the bones that were found scattered at the site of the massacre? If all the bodies were recovered for burial, how do we account for the remains found at the site of the battle? Are they all referring to the same event or have several "legends of the West" merged into one? And what about the names of the chiefs: "Ocean Man?" "Pheasant Rhump?" Is Jack's difficult Victorian newsman's handwriting being deciphered correctly? Subsequent information indicates that both chiefs are known to history.

More details became available in early December 1889 when Jack interviewed a Mr. H. Fegrans of the Royal Geographical Society of Stockholm, Sweden, a member of the survey party who had recently arrived in the city. "He states," Jack recorded, "that the skeletons and carts were not found at Wood Mountain, but on the south slope of the Souris Coteau. Three carts were drawn up in a slough, evidently for the purpose of defence and the attacking party had their position on the hill immediately above, but moved afterward a little to the east toward which position the defenders were exposed. Mr. Fegrans and his companions counted 200 cartridge shells at the two positions held by the aggressors, so it may be assumed that the struggle was a long and severe one. Besides three complete skeletons in the slough there were many other human bones scattered about and the remains of six horses; numerous tin cooking utensils, all riddled with bullets, and several axes were also strewn about the spot. Judging from the appearance of the place the outfit had not been plundered after the fight, which led Mr. Fegrans to believe that the attacking party was composed of white men as Indians would not have killed the horses and would most probably have looted the camp of their victims. The carts were almost honeycombed with bullet holes. They stood at the foot of the slough bank as they had been left on the day of the fight and appeared to be perfectly sound, but when a rancher who thought he could make use of them began handling them they fell to pieces and Mr. Walker's land examining party, of which Mr. Fegrans was a member, secured a month's supply of firewood from the remains. Mr. Fegrans found, among other things, several stone pipes, some of them half filled with tobacco; but the most interesting and probably the most important find, as it may tell the history of the fight, was a small board about a foot long and three and a half inches wide on which were carved over

30 Indian hieroglyphics, Indians, horses and buffaloes being the principal objects delineated. According to this Indian letter the party were out hunting and had made a great deal of pemmican when they met with a party of unfriendly Indians and had a fight in which seven were killed. The slat had been burned almost in two by a prairie fire and the destroyed part somewhat interrupts the thread of the story. There is one thing certain at least, that the little band of hunters was exterminated and their bones left to rot where they fell."

The account ends there and we do not know whether the "Indian letter" was ever "translated" and interpreted in full and linked to any known event or if anybody ever pieced together the details of what the *Free Press* writer calls "the last border fight in the country."

After more than a century the trail is cold, the clues scattered, the witnesses long dead. What actually happened that day long ago on the wind-swept Souris Coteau? Was it a fight of Indian against Indian, some ancient quarrel flaring up for the last time? The Stony, a sub-group of the Assiniboine, had once inhabited parts of southern Saskatchewan and Manitoba, but had been pushed west by incoming tribes. The Gros Ventres, part of the Hidatsa, a Siouan-speaking group living along the Missouri River in western North Dakota, were old enemies of the Stony and likely to fight them on sight. Or was the Stony hunting party ambushed by a gang of murderous white men? Did the Indians who were brought home for burial on their reserve die in some other inci-dent at some other time and place, the two events uniting in the hearsay evidence of unreliable raconteurs long after the event? History has a way of getting mixed up and the late-coming ob-server, looking at mingled fragments of the past, often reaches in-accurate conclusions, turning facts into fiction. How do we know for certain that the victims were Indians? Bones are bones, after all. Perhaps they were a party of white men killed by Indians. Who can say? Modern methods of scientific identification might help, but the bones, by now, are no longer available for study.

Why are we asked to assume that only Indians would have carried away plunder from the victims? A war party, travelling light, might not have been interested in loading themselves with extra baggage and carts and the horses may have been killed because they were in the line of fire during what was clearly a long and hot fight. If the attackers were white men, who were they, where did they come from and where did they go after the battle? So little evidence has come down to us. Indeed, not much evidence was available a mere decade after the supposed event. Journalists like to say that they gather the raw material of history, but in 1889 the story of the battle at the Souris Coteau turned out to be no more than an interesting news story that held the attention of readers for a few days or weeks. It served to remind reporters like Jack that the Old, Wild West was just over the horizon. For us, more than a century on, it is transformed again into an authentic fragment of history.

There was another mystery in the box of letters. Down near the bottom a small, black-covered notebook, an Index-Diary for September 1889. The notebook, which contains a close account of money spent and miles travelled, describes a wagon journey from Winnipeg to Lethbridge via Deloraine, Winlaw, Wood End, Wood Mountain, Frenchman's Creek, Battle Creek, Milk River Coulee, Break Down Camp and McLeod, the North-West Mounted Police establishment in what is now Alberta, with an early detour to Roche Percée, not far from the site of the mysterious massacre. Another detour was made on the 4th of September: "Left Wood End about 8 A.M.—followed dry creek bed all day. Many Indian pipe stems. Great buffalo country. Made detour to find Murder Gulch—found it—remains had all been removed. Lost camp— only found it after dark after going seven miles out. Camp at Badger Hole."

The journal later describes a return by rail to Ottawa via Winnipeg, St. Paul, Minnesota, and "The Soo." In 1889 it had been possible for some years to travel into Alberta by rail. A journey by wagon suggests a tour of inspection along the boundary, possibly by some government official. The road followed seems to roughly parallel the old trail west from Fort Dufferin in Manitoba used by members of the United States and Canadian Boundary Commission in 1873 and by the first contingent of the North-West Mounted Police in their great trek west from Fort Garry to the Old Man's River in 1874. The trail was old even then, having been used by fur traders, buffalo hunters and for centuries by travelling Indians.

No name appears on the journal, but it seems likely that it belonged to W.G. Parmelee, Alice's father, a senior official in the Department of Customs. Mr. Parmelee made many official visits to out-of-the-way places, including a canoe journey with a Hudson's Bay Company party to Moose Factory in the 1890s. In the summers of 1887 and 1888 he travelled as far west as Vancouver and Victoria on official business, on these occasions taking the train. A visit to the boundary survey parties may well have been on his agenda in September 1889.

The handwriting in the small journal looks like Mr. Parmelee's neat banker's hand and he may well have passed on news of the grisly discovery at the Souris Coteau to his future son-in-law, an editor and reporter at the *Free Press*. This, in fact, appears to be what happened. Letters exchanged by Jack and Alice between Ottawa and Winnipeg in October 1889 reveal that Mr. Parmelee was travelling by wagon train in the west in September of that year as a part of the entourage of the the Honourable Mackenzie Bowell. Mr. Bowell, in his ministerial capacity, was travelling west the hard way on a tour of inspection of border arrangements and Alice's father, as a senior civil servant, was along for the bumpy ride over prairie trails in the bone-grinding wagons. His letters home have not been found and the small notebook appears to be the only personal memorial of that interesting and rough journey through the dry border lands to Lethbridge and back, with an interesting detour.

In a letter to Alice dated 30 September 1889 Jack writes: "I saw by the *McLeod Gazette* to hand today that Mr. Bowell and party reached there last Thursday. It did not however state when he would start homeward, so I don't know whether to expect him daily or not." In fact, the party reached Winnipeg about the day the letter to Alice of 30 September was written because a letter written by Jack and mailed to Ottawa on 3 October says that the party "left this morning" on the homeward journey.

Mr. Parmelee, during his one night stopover in Winnipeg, spent several hours with Jack discussing his trip west, but the letter to Alice contains no information "because you will hear all about it from his own lips." They undoubtedly spoke at some length about the massacre at "Murder Gulch," but the correspondence, maddeningly, makes no further reference to the western journey.

Later, at home on Slater Street in Ottawa, Mr. Parmelee received fresh information on the massacre from Jack, written on *Free Press* letter paper. And then, perhaps, while the weary civil servant enjoyed an after dinner nap, the little packet of news slipped from his hand or his pocket and vanished into the secret depths of the sofa, down with the big Queen Victoria pennies, to be retrieved years later by his daughter Julia during spring cleaning operations for the year 1921. Something similar has happened to all of us.

And so the mundane mixes with the monumental, the commonplace with the dramatic, the incomplete materials of history with the insubstantial stuff of myth. What really happened on the Souris Coteau on that terrible day several lifetimes ago? Who were the relentless and merciless attackers? Who were the forlorn defenders who fought to the last man in the hornet swarm of bullets among the wagons on the river bottom? Journalism was unable to find an answer and history misplaced the record. The complete story never appeared in the paper and the true events of that day became entangled with other incidents, yarns, rumours and stories of the time and came down to us fragmented and blurred, like the charred and broken "Indian letter" that the Canadian surveyor found among the broken wagons, scattered cartridge cases and the unburied human remains in a forgotten place called "Murder Gulch" somewhere on the dusty southeastern edge of Saskatchewan.

RITES OF SPRING, 1890

85 Notre Dame
Winnipeg
May 1st 1890

My Darling,
The above is an address line that will be familiar to all your friends after the lapse of a few weeks. It is the Dafoe Mansion. I was reading only this afternoon a letter from you written just about a year ago in which you ask 'Will Castle Dafoe be near the Day Mansion?'

I can answer that question now, My Dear, because today I assumed the new dignity of a householder and next door to me is Mr. E.W. Day, my friend and cribbage opponent. I am duly installed here now and have been working here yesterday afternoon and this afternoon. I am getting the house into something like a habitable condition, but how bare and bleak the rooms are without you. If I only could hear your light step in the next room or your voice upstairs it would make this little house resplendent with warmth and beauty. But you are many hundreds of miles away and so the house must remain desolate for seven long weeks and then, oh sweetheart, I hardly dare to think how happy I will be when I have you here 'at home' with me.

Yesterday was a very busy day. In the early afternoon the carpet was put down and the window blinds put up. By the time they were through I had arrived with the furniture from my room. There was not much trouble in moving though the bookcase bothered me a great deal. Then Scott-Leslie's man brought new furniture and later on Cheapside's man brought some bed clothes, etc. I worked industriously until six o'clock and got my books all replaced in the case, the other furniture in place, the lamps in readiness for action. It was very cold so I put on a roaring fire in the kitchen to take the edge off the dampness in the building. I did not sleep here last night but kept my old quarters and tonight I will slumber beneath my own roof. This afternoon I have been fixing things up, unpacking trunks and doing all sorts of manual labour such a 'making beds,' etc. Downstairs doesn't look bad at all. I have my bookcase in one corner of the room and the rest of that side is taken up with a lounge—and it is a beauty too. The centre table has a picture of my sweetheart on it. There are two easy chairs and a couple of ordinary chairs. I hung two of my large photographs—one a picture of the Press Gallery of 1885 and the other a picture of a group of young fellows in which I figure in the parlour. These are framed in oak and look much better than I thought they would. The other large photograph—the Winnipeg Lacrosse Club of 1889—I have put in the dining room. These pictures are only put up temporarily of course. When you come we will go over the whole thing again.

I am not going to buy much more until you come. I will look around and if I see any nice easy chairs I will get them. I am going to get at least one easy chair warranted big enough for two (for picture hanging emergencies and sentimental moments).

Who is going to be bridesmaid or have you not decided yet? And when is the day to be? It is almost time you took me into your confidence in that respect. I am sure you looked vey nice in that new gown, would that I could see you in it now. But my sweetheart's kiss is not many weeks removed now. And let us hope they will speedily slip away.

Your Jack

Jack was having trouble finding a best man, various friends being unavailable on the proposed date. Finally, on 29 May, he reported success: "I have got a best man! Turner could not come so I fell back on Phil Ross and he is to see me through the ceremony. So there is another arrangement made. I am very glad, Phil and I being as you know very old and warm friends."

While the groom-to-be continued his Pooteresque attempts at home decoration in the North West, Alice, counting the days in Ottawa, prepared her trousseau:

128 Slater St.
Ottawa
June 4th 1890

My Dear Jack
Yesterday was a tantalizing day. There are three mail deliveries a day. Each one brought a letter addressed to me, but none from you. Today's feast almost made amends for yesterday's famine, but I was a little bit anxious yesterday when I did not hear from you for I knew you were not feeling very well. And only one out of the three letters was for me after all. The people in town here do not know which is "Miss" Parmelee and our letters and notes get mixed. One of yesterday's was for Bessie and one for Julia.

Today I received a very handsome present from Mr. and Mrs. Laurence—a water-cooler, the handsomest one I ever saw. Pater has been teasing me all day—says they should have sent a few bottles of water with it for there is none fit to drink in Winnipeg. He expects to make us a visit about August and I have promised him a fine dinner when he comes.

There are three or four other girls in town getting ready to be married among them Miss Shead ("Imperial Louise!") and I am continually meeting them at dressmakers, milliners, etc. and being told that Miss so-and-so has this in her trousseau or Miss Somebody-else has something just like that.

I have not dared to ask for the little card table—it was one of mother's wedding presents and they use it so much. I should like to have it very much, but am afraid that mother values it as highly as I do and would not be willing to part with it.

I packed my trunk of home linen today. I believe I have some housewifely instincts for I just glory in that trunk-full.

Tomorrow I have to make an excursion way down Nelson Street to pay my laundress. I found her after a good deal of trouble—had a hot, dusty walk up Rideau Street then turned to the left down Nelson. I had never been in that part of the town before and was agreeably surprised to find it a cool, shady street shut off from the rest of the city for there were no cross streets. I got quite bewildered for I could find no "next corner" where I had been directed to go and got a child to pilot me. That street was full of children, all sorts and sizes, some very clean, others very dirty but all good natured. The little girl who piloted me had been to a party and came eating her share of the supper as she came. I found the laundress, as I said before, but such a laundress is worth mentioning twice—just the very handsomest, jolliest, plumpest negress I ever saw or anyone else ever saw, I believe. She showed me into a neat little parlour and I almost forgot to come away I was so amused and delighted. Her voice was soft and very musical and she kept breaking into little peals of laughter, throwing up her hands and shaking her head. She offered to do the work I wanted for an absurdly low price because I was "starting new" she said, and it is beautifully done too. I came away quite infected with her light-heartedness and I caught myself smiling at anyone I met on my way up Rideau Street. Well, I have devoted so much time to a description of my lovely laundress that I have no time for anything more—but really, she was charming. Her little daughter is in Bessie's sewing class and is a small copy of her mother.

Only one more letter and then a few days to wait till I see you.

Lovingly,
Alice

As the wedding day approached, even Jack began to feel the first glimmerings of stage fright: "So, Bessie and Lily C. are to be bride's maids; well, you have pretty maids. With the pretty little woman and a good-looking best man (not to mention the transcendent beauty of the groom) we ought to make a pretty sight at St. John's Church. I must plead ignorance of Episcopalian wedding etiquette. I never saw a marriage in a church. All the weddings I have ever witnessed were quiet home affairs where it was not essential to recognize forms. So you must coach me my dear so that I will not make any great blunders. I want to do the thing up in the proper style."

128 Slater St. Ottawa
6 June 1890

Beloved,

I wish you a very good morrow. May you have a pleasant journey with happy thoughts and a cloudless sky.

Yesterday I made another journey down to Nelson St. I was caught in a thunderstorm and had to stay quite a while with my charming black woman. We had a pleasant visit and she gave me a blessing, then sent Jimmy Kees for a cab for me.

Like you, Jack, I cannot write when I will see you so soon. I'll have to fall back on the weather... It is very warm today, the lilacs are in bloom and the rowan trees are sweet with blossoms—they are late for it is well on in June now. It has been threatening rain all day, but looks now as though it is going to clear up.

Are you going to read R.D. Blackmore's "Kit and Kitty" on the way down? Annette liked it, it was so quaint, she said. And what will you read on the way up? Or are you going to be like Mr. White and be annoyed if your wife should read books on the wedding journey?

Oh, if you could hear all the advice I have been given on how to manage a husband you would be an anxious young man. Won't I make you toe the mark! Aren't you afraid?

Dear, I am not going to write more for I cannot give you a real insight into my heart and mind and I don't wish to write more nonsense. Till Friday, Goodbye.

Your Alice.

Of special interest to Alice and Jack was the June 28, 1890 edition of *Town Talk*—"an illustrated weekly devoted to humour, wit, satire, pictorial humour, society, musical, dramatic and sporting news"—a copy of which has survived in the family archive down to the present time. Jack, for a time, had been gossip and sports correspondent to the weekly effusion, but he had refrained from attempting wit or humour, which, in *Town Talk* was clearly designed to produce groans: "Winnipeg doctors charge such heavy fees for medical attendance merely to follow the divine injunction 'Physician, heel thyself'"—A city cornet player who was engaged to play at the Bijou the other evening in place of a regular performer quietly remarked to Frank Campbell that he was a 'sub' to toot"—A Winnipeg Q.C. has stopped his subscription to the St. John's College magazine because it advertises the products of a brewery. This is one way of putting down beer."

The featured cartoon—called "the big cut" in those days— comments on the recent arrival of women in the workplace. The scene is an office. A young woman works busily at her typewriter. Across the office the boss is gazing in her direction with a look that can mean only one thing. Cupid is there too, fitting an arrow into his bow. We are in at the birth of sexual harassment in the workplace.

In the social and personal section of the magazine we learn that Mrs. William Bannatyne has gone to Europe, Mr. and Mrs. J.A.M. Aikins have returned from the East and that "a large number of ladies and gentlemen are preparing to go to Rat Portage to enjoy a few days among the islands."

Another social item catches the eye in this ancient and crumbling copy of *Town Talk*:

"The return of Mr. J.W. Dafoe with his bride this week was signalized by the presentation to the happy couple of a magnificent silver epergne by his fellow workers on the *Free Press*, which gave them opportunity to welcome him home. *Town Talk*, to which Mr. Dafoe was once a valued contributor, modestly proffered its best of good wishes accompanied by a handsome marble clock and some brilliant and beautiful gems of poetry in which the newlywed pair were asked to

Remember Town Talk
When they looked at the clock

And the sincere hope that this would furnish all the "tick" needed on their journey through life. John is a hard-working, conscientious newspaper man, a good thinker, an excellent writer, a great favourite with all who know him, and he ought to make a model husband. His lacrosse friends also made him a valuable present and many friends added to the long list of presents received in the East."

Alice to Jack, Spring 1890: "I have had a singularly happy life so far and somehow I feel that it is going to continue happy to the end."

Jack, for his part, had already made it clear that he would not miss being single: "I am prepared to admit that I never found the alleged liberty of the single young man at all pleasant. With me it was marked by morbidity, bad temper, restlessness and despondency. I expect to be as happy and contented a mortal as ever breathed. If I am not, it will be my own fault."

Jack and Alice seem a bit ill-at-ease in the wedding photograph taken by the celebrated firm of William Notman and Son
"Photographers to the Queen" at the start of the honeymoon
trip. Alice clutches her reticule and fixes her gaze on something
off to her right, while Jack leans on a chair back and gazes pen-
sively into the middle distance. It seems like an awkward start
to married life. On the other hand, it may simply be an indica-
tion of the overwhelming nature of the average Victorian honeymoon. They would soon hit their stride and carry on happily for
another half century.

GO EAST, YOUNG MAN

Jack and Alice settled into marital bliss at their little house at 85 Notre Dame—pronounced the American way "Noter Dame"—a short walk from the *Free Press* office. The rent was $14 a month. Jack's pay at the *Free Press* was $8.00 a week, augmented by free-lance payments. His young brother Wallace had moved into the spare bedroom and was attending high school and doing well. Alice met and liked the next door neighbours, Jack's friends the Days, and she and Jack joined in the cribbage and euchre games and attended and gave dinner parties. Jack even submitted to Matins with Alice at Holy Trinity church, although he complained that he found the Anglican Book of Common Prayer "a regular Chinese puzzle." They went for picnics along the river on summer Sunday afternoons, he took her on excursions in a boat, they attended plays and concerts and Alice began to get used to being on her own when Jack put in his long hours at the newspaper. Fortunately, she was an avid reader. Coal-oil lamps were still in use for reading after dark in the Dafoe Mansion, but one of Winnipeg's two electric light companies was putting up poles and wires along Notre Dame Avenue and the newlyweds would soon be enjoying the full splendour of the incandescent light bulb.

Life was rosy in Winnipeg, but Jack was well aware that the *Free Press* did not, after all, represent the pinnacle or apogee of journalistic endeavour. He remained ambitious. In a letter to Alice, visiting in Ottawa at Christmas 1891, he passed on news of George Ham who was "feeling blue" in the East and, as he put it, "would sooner be in Winnipeg sawing wood." "I wonder," Jack wrote, "what it is that makes us all so fond of this city. It would cut me a good deal to leave this town, but I wouldn't hesitate to do it. I have got to get a good deal higher on the ladder than I am now before I will begin to be satisfied and I have got into a cul-de-sac at the FP—at the best I can only get D.J. Beaton's place if he should go into railroading and then it will simply be that I will work like a horse making bullets and firing them so that W.F. Luxton may get the credit and the cash. Young Beaton tells me that his father is profoundly dissatisfied. And no wonder. He is easily the ablest man on our paper; I don't believe that there is a finer editorial writer in Canada and he gets perhaps a third of what he is worth while W.F.L. draws $5,200 a year and his manager J.B. Somerset two or three thousand. For myself, I am not dissatisfied. I am young and my income is a tidy one, but just the same I feel capable of doing better work than I am doing on the FP. Consul Taylor, not knowing I had written it, praised very highly one of my editorials. I was quite pleased. I would like to do editorial work on a paper where I could strike out from the shoulder."

Unknown to Alice, but probably a nagging worry to Jack, was the fact that the *Free Press*, in spite of apparent success and prosperity, was in serious trouble. Jack's chief, W.F. Luxton, was gradually losing control of the paper he had co-founded with John Kenny in 1872. From its earliest days the *Free Press* had taken an independent line. With Luxton's Reform banner nailed to the mast the paper obtained a wide readership, but was not a big money-maker. After a possibly ill-advised expansion in 1885, Luxton was forced to incorporate as a joint stock venture with a board of directors.

By 1888 the financial situation was critical and in September of that year the *Free Press* accepted a five-year loan of $26,000 from Donald A. Smith, the future Lord Strathcona, for which that wily gnome of finance received 796 shares with a face value of $79,600 as collateral. Not long after this, Smith's friend Sir William Van Horne, the new President of the CPR, bought a *Free Press* rival, *The Call*, for $35,000. Like Scrooge and Marley, Van Horne and Smith proceeded to spin their web around the unsuspecting Luxton. Early in 1889 the capital stock of the *Free Press* was increased to $133,500 with 335 shares being turned over to Van Horne in exchange for the assets of *The Call*. The *Free Press* was later loaned $40,000, possibly by Smith, to buy out another rival, *The Sun*. Luxton, who had forgotten to bring his long spoon to this supper with the devil, was jubilant—but not for long. He was soon to be aware that he no longer controlled the paper and began to squirm under the pressure from his new partners. Smith and Van Horne, who had obtained control of the *Free Press* in order to advance the interests of the CPR, were prepared to push Luxton overboard, which they would do without ceremony in 1893 after subjecting him to a bit more financial torture.

By late 1891 it was clear to Jack that the time had come to make a change. Once again he was trying his hand at literature. In a letter to Alice, who was spending Christmas with her parents in Ottawa and Waterloo, Quebec, he drew her attention to his latest piece of fiction: "I suppose you saw my story in the last *Dominion Illustrated*. There are just a few proof-reading slips in it. I was somewhat surprised to see that it read so well. I really think it is the best thing I have ever done."

Alice, in Ottawa, was slowly recovering from the horrors of the trip from Winnipeg. She had been sick on the train, only able to keep down the apples Jack had put in her suitcase. The days of fasting, however, had made her quite slim: "I don't recognize myself in the glass." On top of being ill, she had suffered the unwelcome advances of a fellow passenger. "The only 'mash' I made," she reported, "was a young Frenchman I took to be a Jesuit priest who tried most persistently to strike up an acquaintance and was much distressed because I would not allow him to get me whisky or tea or coffee or anything."

Back in Winnipeg the weather was even worse than usual. "It has grown very cold," Jack reported. "On getting up I found the water in the basin frozen solid and ice formed in the jug." Nevertheless, he looked on the bright side: "A lively scrub in ice cold water made me feel fine." He had left a window open. That was a problem in Winnipeg. You could keep the window shut and suffocate, or open it and freeze.

Literature and the Winnipeg weather were not his only concerns however. There was momentous news of another sort as well. Jack had learned that a group of Quebec Liberals were negotiating the purchase of the *Montreal Herald*, an English language newspaper that had been established during the first decade of the nineteenth century. The paper had fallen on hard times in recent years, but was about to attempt a comeback as a Liberal organ with E.G. O'Connor, Jack's old chief at the *Star*, as publisher. Jack had sent a query to Wilfrid Laurier and had received an interesting reply which he passed on to Alice: "I enclose you a letter from Mr. Laurier that will interest you. If I can get the management of the *Herald* I will take it. I feel in my bones that I could make it 'go.' I intend to write to Mr. Laurier tomorrow. Keep mum on the subject excepting to your parents. You can tell them if you want to." Alice's reply, mailed on the 23rd was enthusiastic: "I was indeed interested in the enclosure to your letter of the 19th. I was so excited I could hardly read it. Mr. Laurier answered your letter very promptly, did he not?" The Parmelees, in fact, had known all about the Montreal developments and had been happily discussing Jack's chances of getting the editorship of the *Herald*, even before Alice had arrived in Ottawa.

Laurier's letter, which still exists in the family archive, made it pretty clear that Jack had only to ask. "The *Herald* is in liquidation," the Liberal leader wrote. "I have reason to believe that a company is now being organized with the view of buying the paper and continuing it as a Liberal paper. Still if you felt inclined to come back to this province and to take hold of the *Herald* I am pretty sure that it would be possible to give you a preference. I remember very well the good work you used to do as parliamentary correspondent of the *Star.*" Laurier added that he would soon be visiting Manitoba, hinting at a possible meeting. Jack must have felt that the *Herald* job was in the bag. And so it was. Within a few weeks they would break up their home in Winnipeg, pack Jack's books, the furniture, the epergne, the clock and the photograph of the lacrosse team and make the journey to the East.

Alice was expecting her first child in May 1892 and while Jack and his brother Rance, who had accompanied them, organized a home in Montreal, Alice would settle in with her parents in Ottawa, arriving in Montreal in time for her confinement.

The revived *Herald* was launched at the end of April under its new publisher and editor, who nailed their colours to the mast with the following announcement: "Politically the *Herald* will be an Independent Liberal newspaper. To the best of its ability it will be an exponent of the principles of Liberalism laid down by those stainless leaders Louis-Hippolyte La Fontaine, Luther Holton, Antoine-Aimé Dorion and Alexander Mackenzie. It will stand for purity in public life; for the widest freedom of trade; for a broad patriotism based on confidence in the resources of our country. It will endeavour always to be thoroughly Canadian." With these ringing words the *Herald* was reborn.

The other baby arrived on 29 May and mother and child soon rejoined the Parmelees in Ottawa. By July Alice was anxious to return to Jack in Montreal. "I get the *Herald* regularly," she wrote on 3 July, "and enjoy the reading of it. Mother and I were here alone with Baby. Dr. Wright came in Friday afternoon to see how the medicine had worked and thought Baby was looking alright again. He says she is a bonny baby and that her large nose indicates intellect. Pater suggests that Baby be named Mary Alice."

Alice and baby Mary Alice soon joined Jack and his brother in Montreal and they began to settle into their new life. Things were going well at the *Herald*. Circulation was increasing week by week and Jack was assembling a strong staff. He was sharpening his editorial pen on themes—free trade and Canadian nationalism—that would inspire him all his days. The *Herald* seemed set to flourish. Then disaster struck on 27 March 1893. Alice was visiting the family in Ottawa and Jack told her the sad story in a letter sent on 1 April:

> Got home from Ottawa on Monday at noon. Worked in the office all afternoon. Took tea with the O'Connors and afterwards sat in Mr. O'C's study and discussed the estimates with him for the ensuing year. Got a telephone message at 10:30 that the *Herald* was on fire and got down there in about two minutes. By midnight was hard at work on an edition.

This was the second fire to strike the old newspaper in recent years and this time as the smoke cleared it looked as if there might be no revival. Then Hugh Graham and the *Star* came to the rescue, offering office space and the use of presses to their Liberal rival, which was broad-minded of Graham because the *Herald* had been unstinting in its ridicule of the *Star*'s support of Tory trade policies. Jack, meanwhile, was having a busy week:

> Tuesday—up at nine. Spent all forenoon with Mr. Halton and Mr. O'Connor and all the afternoon in bossing the fixing up of our quarters in the Star building. Worked all night on the edition and went home with Mr. Menzies our foreman between five and six o'clock.
>
> Wednesday—Up at noon. Busy as a bee all afternoon. Took tea with Mr. O'C. Went home with Menzies in the morning.

Thursday—Downtown at noon. Spent much of the afternoon at business office in consultation and followed the work of the issue of the paper through until it was on the street in good season.

All the people are very brave over the calamity. I have surprised myself at the way I stood the fire. I wasn't rattled and was not nervous and I wasn't blue (barring one or two times when I could have sat down and wept when I thought of all our hard work going up in smoke}.

Alice herself had first responded to news of the fire in a letter written from Ottawa on the morning of 28 March: "The only thing I keep thinking of over and over again is how thankful I am that your office was moved down from the third floor. I was asleep when your telegram came last night and they did not show it to me until this morning. It was good of you to send the message dear for I should have been terrified if I had seen the newspaper account first." She was anxious to join him in Montreal as soon as possible: "Just telegraph me 'all right come' and I'll do the rest."

Soon the *Herald*, a bit tottery and bruised, seemed to be back on its feet and Jack was once more in the thick of the political battle that would put the federal Liberal party under Laurier back into power after 18 years in the wilderness. In his old age Jack would look back on the campaign leading up to that 1896 victory for the Liberal combination of Laurier and Israel Tarte with pleasure and an undiminished feeling of excitement and pride: "It was for the Liberals a stimulating and cheering campaign. The stars in their courses fought for us. All the breaks of the game came our way. The distracted Conservatives, following the death of Sir John Macdonald, had four changes of leadership in as many years. The difficulties which had accumulated during many years of office were beyond solution. I was young, still in my twenties, and I put everything I had into the campaign short of public speaking—a vice I had not yet acquired. I travelled the country with the party campaigners from Laurier down; sat in with the party strategists; was busy with propaganda."

Years later Jack was still thrilled to recall that campaign. "I have many lively recollections of that struggle and particularly of a meeting in Montreal which remains in my memory as the most completely satisfactory event of the kind that I have ever experienced. It was to be the opening gun in the campaign in Montreal; and we had grave doubts as to whether we could fill Windsor Hall, the party not having had much luck in the city in previous contests. When the night came, the meeting only failed of being one of the greatest ever addressed by Laurier by the inability of the thousands who were outside to get into the hall. As Laurier rose to speak to the crowded audience he threw up his hands and said, 'Can this be Tory Montreal?' I do not think any of my experiences in later political campaigns ever quite matched the night of June 23, 1896, when we were able to figure out before midnight a definite Liberal majority."

It was a bright new day for the Liberal party, but the fire and the struggle to restore the *Herald*'s fortunes brought hard times for the paper. In 1894 Jack replied to a friend in Ottawa who had written about a job on the *Herald* that he had better stay where he was for "The ghost of the *Herald* is hardly walking these days." It appears that Jack was keeping the bad news from Alice. In a letter written on 5 July 1894 from Hill Head near Lachute where the family would spend the summers during their Montreal years, Alice wrote happily about his approaching visit. "I am so glad that the *Herald* is doing so well at last. That will do you more good than a trip to the seaside. But don't forget that you are coming here for a whole week before we go back just the same." By 1895, however, the financial backers of the paper had reached their limit and the *Herald* was sold. In August of that year Jack left the paper.

Once again Hugh Graham was there to lend a hand. Jack returned to the *Star* organization, becoming editor of Graham's

Family Herald and *Weekly Star* with the understanding that he would not write about politics in the paper. He was free, however, to continue his work for the Liberals in his own time.

The call to action was not long in coming. Jack had been present at the political meeting at Portage la Prairie in August 1889 when D'Alton McCarthy and others had called for the abolition of separate Roman Catholic schools and French language rights, guaranteed under the Manitoba Act of 1870. The subsequent repeal of these provisions by the Manitoba government of Thomas Greenway had created a windstorm that had followed Jack into the East, becoming a national issue that threatened to seriously damage the structure of Confederation. Two decisions of the British Privy Council, in 1892 and 1895, upheld the validity of the Manitoba law, but also upheld the federal government's power to restore the lost rights through remedial legislation. This task fell to the lot of the Conservative Prime Minister, the aged Orangeman Mackenzie Bowell, one of a miscellany of Conservative leaders who attempted to govern after the passing of John A. Macdonald in 1891. Remedial legislation proposed by Bowell early in 1896 led to turmoil in the Conservative party, followed by Bowell's resignation as prime minister. The issue became a major bone of contention in the election of 1896, which the Conservatives fought under a new leader, Charles Tupper.

In February of that year Jack had published a long letter on the Schools Question in *The Week* in which he argued that remedial legislation, as proposed by the federal government, would lead, inevitably, to religious and racial strife. Laurier's "sunny way" of compromise and conciliation was the best way to deal with the problem, the answer, Jack wrote, "which every man in Canada, Catholic or Protestant, can follow with honour." When the election came later in the year it brought with it a firestorm of religious controversy over the issue. The Western priest Father Lacombe sent a letter threatening Laurier with the wrath of the clergy. Jack arranged for this incendiary letter to obtain wide circulation in the press. The destructive religious controversy that followed was later cooled by the diplomatic intervention of the Vatican. As Jack later wrote, "The bishops destroyed themselves by their violence. Rome does not lightly quarrel with governments and prime ministers. Laurier had never again to face the embattled bishops, which is not the same thing as saying that they ceased to take a hand in politics."

Under the new Liberal government a compromise was agreed to between Prime Minister Laurier and Premier Greenway in which limited church and language rights were restored in qualifying schools in Manitoba. The ill-feeling created by the controversy would, however, simmer for much of the next century.

Jack edited the *Family Herald* and *Weekly Star* for six years and during that time the circulation rose from fifty thousand to over one hundred thousand. The paper was read across Canada in cities, towns and, especially, on farms, but was essentially a farm paper. It contained horticultural advice, tips on the care of cattle, recipes, sewing patterns and material of special interest to families. It featured, as well, short stories, non-fiction, domestic and foreign news of interest and items designed to entertain and educate children and young people. Many Canadian writers of the period, including Charles G.D. Roberts and Duncan Campbell Scott, contributed short stories and serials to the paper. Jack got Alice's sister Annette to conduct competitions and write book reviews. He wrote book reviews and causeries himself, one, published in November 1895, marking the centenary of the birth of John Keats. "The younger poets of the United States," Jack noted, "owe more to Keats than to his disciples. This is true of our Canadian poets too; the influence of Keats has been strong upon them. Mr. Lampman, for example, though an original and true singer, reveals on every page the fountain head of his inspiration." He may have been thinking wistfully, as well, of his own abandoned efforts as a poet.

There was something in the weekly for everyone. There was a science column and a "how to" feature. A young Halifax lawyer, Robert L. Borden, contributed a column of legal advice. Years later, when Borden, a Conservative, was serving as prime minister in a wartime Union government made up of Conservatives and Liberals he would include Jack in the Canadian delegation to the 1919 peace conference and arrange the tour of the Western Front with the Canadian General Sir Arthur Currie that would provide him with material for his book *Over the Canadian Battlefields*. His friend Borden was also involved in the offer of a knighthood that Jack felt bound to decline.

During his second stint at the *Star* he had another brief run at the life of a "man of letters." He appears to have written no more poetry after 1890, but he did turn his hand to fiction, with some little success. An issue of *The Herald* published in May 1895 features a short story, "The Loup-Garou, Written for the *Herald* by J.W.D." The story, a melodramatic tale of demonic possession in the backwoods of New France, has quite as much blood, thunder and gore as Jack's boyhood poems, and may have been intended for younger readers. Other J.W. Dafoe stories appeared in *The Canadian Magazine*, a Toronto journal that attempted from the 1880s until after the First World War, to emulate American magazines such as the *Atlantic* and *Harper's*. Stories published in *The Canadian Magazine* include "By Niagara's Banks," an adventure story of the War of 1812, published with illustrations by Fred H. Brigden, and "A Call from the Gorge," a tragic tale of life and death among the river men and lumberjacks on the Ottawa which may have owed something to his father's years in the lumber camps and is the best thing of this kind that he wrote. The final story appeared in *The Canadian Magazine* in 1901, the year he returned to the West. These stories may have been intended as "pot-boilers," written to help augment an insufficient income and help support a growing family or they may represent a final effort to make a mark in the world of literature. By 1901, however, it is clear that he had made up his mind. His career would be in journalism and in the struggle for Canadian nationhood. His stories had been generally well received, but their author understood his limitations as a creator of literary work. Unlike many newsmen, who hopefully keep a half-finished novel in a bottom drawer, he tried his hand at fiction early and discovered that his true calling was journalism. And to journalism he would dedicate the rest of his life.

Years later he would speak of that special and often misunderstood calling to a group of students at the University of Manitoba. "A journalist," he told them, "is hardly an authority upon anything—unless perhaps upon the appraisal of the drift of public opinion. His writings on economics are likely to be greeted by your professor of economics with a polite snort. Eminent lawyers disagree with his constitutional pronouncements. Preachers do not subscribe to his theological views. Transportation experts regard his comment on freight rates as wholly uninformed; financial magnates consider his ventures into the mazes of finance as the triumph of reckless ignorance over prudence. And yet, in spite of all these limitations, the journalist must go forward laying hands upon these and other mysteries with a sort of reckless courage; and unless he is to fail he must out of his half-knowledge and his intuitions, his sense of values and his knowledge of life, tell a story which may not be accurate but is still true and which does not altogether lack suggestive power."

As the century drew to a close he was increasingly aware that the *Family Herald* and *Weekly Star* were not ideal for his talents. He had done well, the *Herald* had a large national circulation and he could probably go on editing it until he was an old man ready to retire, but he was looking for a job that would bring him into the thick of the political struggle in the years ahead. The right-leaning *Star* was not the paper for him. He was grateful to Hugh

Graham for giving him a chance to make a living in Montreal and he had enjoyed working as Graham's confidential secretary, assisting the publisher on various special projects, but as he entered his thirties he increasingly felt the need to get on with his real work. As the century drew to a close he was looking about him for new opportunities. He had also discovered that he missed the West. He had not seen his family in Manitoba for years. If the right job could be found there he would grab it.

His marriage had proved to be a happy one, approaching the Ibsenite ideal. He and Alice had a growing family. Mary Alice, born in 1892, had been joined by Edwin (Ted) in 1894, by Dorothy in 1895, by John (another Jack) in 1897 and by Marcella in 1898. Other children would follow in the years to come: Elizabeth in 1900, William in 1902 and Sydney in 1904. William and Sydney would both die in infancy. Philip Van Rensselaer (Van), born in 1905, would complete the family.

Jack's brother Rance was living with the family and learning the newspaper business while he courted his future wife, Alice's maid, Mary McLeod, on summer weekends at Hill Head. Brother Wallace had joined the *Free Press* as a reporter in 1890. By 1896 he was a Parliamentary reporter at the *Ottawa Journal*, joining Jack as a news editor at the *Montreal Star* in 1899. Wallace would later return to the Ottawa Press Gallery, representing the *London Daily Mail*, the *Montreal Witness* and the *Toronto Star*.

The nineteenth century move toward its end with Laurier in power in Ottawa and war brewing in South Africa. Jack plodded on at the *Star*, but he was feeling restless and looking about for a chance to move on.

He had been looking for more freelance opportunities, as he informed Alice in a letter written to her at Hill Head on 7 June, 1898. Alone in the city, he had been sweltering in the early summer heat, seeking cool breezes on Fletcher's Field near Mount Royal, but work was calling. "Today," he wrote, "I have been more industrious, but am so far behind that I'll have to get in some thundering big licks tomorrow. I wrote an article last week for the *New York Independent* on the Alaskan Boundary. They accepted it, but sent it back to be re-cast in accordance with the latest developments. I did it and sent it off again this evening. It will be a signed article and as the *Independent* is a paper of fine standing its publication will give a boost to my ambition to become a recognized writer for foreign papers on Canadian subjects. I tried to jolly the *Atlantic Monthly* into giving me a commission to write on a suggested Canadian subject, but got turned down politely."

In August 1899, while the family enjoyed country life at Hill Head, Jack fought the heat and continued his program of self-improvement: "Today," he wrote to Alice, "I gratified a wish of long standing by buying the first volume of the Temple Edition of the works of Michel de Montaigne. It is not creditable to me that, at my age, Montaigne should be, to me, an undiscovered country; and I propose removing this cause of reproach. There are in all six volumes, but I'll buy them volume by volume as I want them." He had finished reading *Peter Ibbetson* coming home on the train from Hill Head. "It is very queer," he wrote," but I found it interesting. None of George du Maurier's work as a writer will last, though, clever as it is." Another book that he had found wanting had been summarily tossed out the train window.

In July 1900 the family, as usual, was enjoying the summer days at Hill Head, with Jack coming down, if he could, by train on Saturday night. There was serious illness in the neighbourhood. The local doctor declined to give the disease a name, although it was likely typhoid. Symptoms included fever, purging and vomiting. Alice was taking no chances, as she assured Jack in a letter written in early July: "I used six pails of ashes, a package of chloride of lime and some permanganate of potash about the house today and it all seems quite sweet and wholesome. This is the month one needs to be especially careful about such matters.

The children all seem very well. Marcella included Dan the horse in her prayers tonight, putting him right after Papa."

Alice had been reading Thomas Hardy's *The Return of the Native* and enjoying the novelty of country life. "The hen," she reported in a letter to Jack, "has given up trying to crow or else I have been sleeping too late to hear her."

The family was back at Hill Head in July 1901, but it would be their last holiday in that delightful country retreat. As summer settled in Jack had received a job offer that would prove to be too good to refuse.

INTO MY KINGDOM

On 3 August 1901 Jack Dafoe found himself cooling his heels in the luxurious Gananoque Inn on the shore of the St. Lawrence River "Among the Thousand Islands," summer playground of the .rich. He had been summoned there by Clifford Sifton, Minister of the Interior in the Laurier government, who had recently stepped forward as the new proprietor of Jack's former employer, the *Manitoba Free Press*.

Earlier in the summer Jack had accepted the position of Editor of the *Free Press* and he had travelled to Gananoque from Montreal for extensive consultations with his new chief. Mr. Sifton, however, was tied up in meetings with Interior Department officials. He would fit Jack in when the government meetings concluded. Meanwhile, the new editor did his best to enjoy his unexpected holiday—after first ascertaining that his hotel bill would be picked up by the *Free Press*. His only problem, he reported in a letter to Alice, was that he had forgotten to bring a book.

Clifford Sifton had acquired the *Free Press* in 1898 after Hugh John Macdonald, son of the late prime minister, had been unable to raise enough money to effect its purchase from its former owners, Donald A. Smith and Sir William Van Horne, the CPR men having concluded that, even with a CPR publicity man as editor, the paper had little public relations value for the railroad. Even under a new editor, A.J. Magurn, the paper did not please and it was quietly sold to Sifton, a former Manitoba

Attorney General who was now a powerful minister in the Laurier government.

The sale took place under such a cloud of secrecy that Editor Magurn was at first unaware that Sifton was his new chief, responding rudely to suggestions from the new owner as to how the paper should be run. Sifton soon decided that Magurn had to go and he began his search for a new editor. Jack's candidacy was soon under active consideration, the first contact being made in January 1901. It is likely that Sifton remembered Jack as a member of the Manitoba Press Gallery after 1886 and he undoubtedly knew of his more recent work in Montreal at the *Herald* and the *Star*. In a letter to a Liberal colleague in Manitoba Sifton paid glowing tribute to his prospective editor. Dafoe, Sifton wrote, "is well and thoroughly known to the leading Liberals of Ontario and Quebec, and in respect of his ability and character there is no journalist in Canada who stands higher. It is a good deal to say that the Liberals so regard him notwithstanding the fact that he has been for many years on the *Montreal Star*." It is also probable that Wilfrid Laurier put in a good word for Jack, pointing to his valiant efforts at the ill-starred *Montreal Herald* and in the smoke-filled rooms at election time in 1896. Jack, however, was on pins and needles for much of the early part of 1901 as he waited for a firm offer to be made.

An ardent but independent-minded Liberal, Sifton was also an astute man of business and he wanted his newspaper, which had been a poor earner in the past, to become a viable financial enterprise under the new regime. He was aware that the *Family Herald* and *Weekly Star* had gained a vast national circulation under Dafoe's editorship. The paper, in fact, had been a money spinner for the *Star* organization. The *Free Press* had its own weekly edition which would, he hoped, become in time the pre-eminent farm newspaper in Western Canada, a major source of revenue and a political hurdy-gurdy for the causes, national and local, in which he was interested. In Dafoe, he felt, he had found an editor with ideas and capacities similar to his own. Over the next twenty-five years they would be in regular communication, not always agreeing on everything, but respecting each other's opinions and always united in the desire to make the *Free Press* the voice of Western Canada and the defender of Western interests.

To oversee the financial side of his newspaper, Sifton has acquired the services of the formidable E.H. Macklin, an accountant at the *Toronto Globe*. The Macklin-Dafoe partnership was expected to make the *Free Press* a powerful force and secure Western Canada for the Liberal cause, although the paper would maintain an independent position with regard to policy. At the same time, it was hoped, the *Free Press* would make some money for Sifton. When the editorship of the *Free Press* was finally offered, Jack recalled in later life, "it only took me the millionth part of a second to accept."

The news of Jack's appointment came through in late June and by 3 July he was writing to Alice at Hill Head with a report on his last days at the *Star*: "I let the cat out of the bag today and as a result haven't done much work—fellows dropping in on me from all over the office to talk it over. I saw Mr. Graham this morning. He was very nice, but I could see he was disturbed at the news. I told him my views very frankly, said that I was perfectly satisfied with his treatment of me but felt that I owed it to myself to do the best work that was in me and that I could not do so at the *Star*. Fred Williams wired the news to the *Winnipeg Tribune* so the people there will know it tonight. Poor Magurn! I can't help but feel sorry for him. He got his notification last week. I forgot to say that when I got to the office yesterday I had a letter from the Manitoba Free Press Co. confirming the verbal arrangements arrived at with C.S. I wrote at once accepting it."

While Alice remained with the children at Hill Head, Jack, with the assistance of Mary McLeod, organized the packing of their furniture, books, pictures and other household effects in their rented Montreal home on Shuter Street for removal to Manitoba. Alice and the children would stay at Hill Head while he went west to settle in at the FP and establish a home for them in Winnipeg. He would return to Quebec in the autumn, collect the family, and bring them to their new home in the West.

The Dafoes of Killarney, who had not seen Alice and Jack for almost a decade, were in a frenzy of excitement about the forthcoming return to Manitoba. Others seemed to think that Jack was out of his mind to leave a perfectly good job in Montreal for a dubious position in what was, to them, the middle of nowhere. "The Elcomes," Jack informed Alice in a letter, "continue to be flabbergasted over our Winnipeg move. I tell them they did not make so much fuss over me when I went far off long ago, and it must be you that they are so fond of—which is, I guess, pretty much the fact. I don't believe you know how dearly beloved you are by the Dafoes and their kindred unto the third and fourth generation. I married to please myself and in doing that I delighted all my friends."

In a letter to Alice written on 17 August Jack announced his arrival in Winnipeg: "Got here all right today at noon—six hours late." He was a bit taken aback at first to discover that several old acquaintances he encountered at the station and on the street could not place him. "I haven't been around much," he told Alice, "but I fancy if I wanted to see the city in disguise I could do so just by going out as I am." The ice broke at Erzinger's barber shop "where Si the head barber spotted me by my voice."

After sprucing up at Erzinger's he presented himself at the *Free Press* where he met several old friends, including his old boss, Walter Payne, and, for the first time, E.H. Macklin with whom he would have an often stormy relationship for the next thirty years.

Two days later the change of editorship was announced in the paper. "As the result," he informed Alice, "I got a good many calls—Jim Tees, Duncan McIntyre of the *Tribune*, John Gail (who doesn't look like me anymore now that I am getting into the fat man's club), Chief McRae, Sanford Evans (the Editor of the *Telegram* and my deadly rival), J.P. Robertson, Jim Hooper, etc, etc." An out-of-town visitor was an old acquaintance from Montreal, the poet William Henry Drummond, in town to give a public reading of his popular "Habitant" poems. "No doubt there will be a crowd," Jack predicted. "There are so few things of this sort here that when there is one everybody goes."

Jack was living at the Leland hotel and spending a lot of time at the office, which he described as "cold and cheerless." The work, however, was totally absorbing and he found it hard to stay away from his desk, occasionally missing a meal and having to slip out to Frank Mariaggi's hotel restaurant on "Newspaper Row" at midnight for a "quick snack." One Saturday evening, with the office shut and the Leland's otherwise comfortable lobby full of "drunken men," he went for a stroll among the crowds on Main Street, stopping to listen to street-corner orators and hucksters. Main Street, which he remembered as a mudhole, had recently been paved and you could now go for a walk and not arrive home "drenched in slops." The rough frontier town he had left in the early nineties was becoming a real city.

"Coming back to the hotel I had a chat with Mr. John Mather of Ottawa who was waiting to go East. Mr. Mather is President of the Free Press Co. He seems to be a pleasant old gentleman. A.J. Magurn quarrelled with him bitterly, but I do not imagine that I shall have any trouble getting along with him."

Things were going well at the office too: "Matters are running along nicely: and everybody feeling gay. The old ship FP is beginning to find herself again." Jack looked around him and felt that the curtain was finally rising on the second act of his life. He was 35 years old, his youth was passing and his years of wandering and apprenticeship were over. "I am more and more pleased that I came West," he wrote to Alice in early September. "At last I feel that I have come into my kingdom." At the end of his life he looked back and relished the moment once again: "I had landed the very position that I had often dreamed of occupying, for I had found after my return to Montreal that I had given my heart to the West. I have said that I have had a fortunate life and the crowning proof is that after some few years of changing experience I found the position and the task to which I could give all my remaining years."

Within a few weeks of his arrival he bought a large, newly-built brick house on Spence Street, not far from where he and Alice had lived during the first years of their marriage. The open prairie was near, but he could walk to the office and the new Isbister School was around the corner, just right for the children. As September advanced he was busy filling the new "Dafoe Mansion" with their furniture, pictures and books; buying a furnace and a range for the kitchen; seeing about a wood and coal supply; establishing contact with Hardy and Buchanan, the local grocers; putting in electric lights and a telephone. He kept Alice informed on his progress. The house would be ready to live in when she and the children arrived in Winnipeg.

Beside the house there was an extra half lot in which, in years to come, the family would create a skating rink every winter. There would be circuses on the lawn under the trees on summer days in the early years of the new century. The city would grow up around them, far out onto what in 1901 had been bare prairie. They would live there until the children were grown. Jack's parents would spend their last years as guests at 509 Spence Street and there would always be room for relations, near and distant, who were passing through town or in need of a meal or a bed. One old uncle, Harvey Dafoe, formerly of Zion's Hill, was a frequent visitor who would arrive unannounced and stay for long periods, amusing the children with his ability to play the bones and dance country jigs. One autumn, weary of Manitoba, he de-camped to Vancouver to stay with Jack's sister, Edith. Later, on Christmas Eve, just as the family was sitting down to dinner, the doorbell rang. Jack opened the front door and there was Uncle Harvey with his luggage. "I'd rather frizz than drown," he said.

Two sons—Ted in the cavalry and later in the Royal Flying Corps and young Jack in the infantry—would leave Spence Street to fight in the First World War, meeting their father at his London hotel at Christmas 1918 and dining in his suite because Jack, who was recovering from serious wounds sustained at Passchendaele, being only a private, was not allowed to enter the hotel dining room. Van, the youngest son, would serve in the Second World War.

The girls, all clever and well read like their parents, would do well at school, Marcella and Elizabeth graduating from the University of Manitoba, Elizabeth becoming university librarian and Marcella following private intellectual interests, including assistance to her father as researcher for his biography of Clifford Sifton. Mary Alice, the eldest daughter, would go on to occupy senior positions in the Anglican Church and the YWCA. Dorothy would become a teacher.

Missing Hill Head, the family would at first spend summers with the Dafoe grandparents at Killarney, later establishing a summer retreat at Ponemah on the western shore of Lake Winnipeg. It was still being enjoyed by family members in the twenty-first century, more than a hundred years after Manitoba had become home.

In late August and early September 1901, while Jack prepared to travel east to collect Alice and the children, he explored the city he had left almost a decade before and found it greatly changed. "I have poked about the city considerably," he informed Alice, "and it certainly has improved. Many of the residential streets have been asphalted and boulevarded and the houses are less of the shack order than of yore. Even the small frame houses have foundations. I went for a stroll up Balmoral way on Sunday morning. Old 359 Notre Dame Street [the number had been changed from 85] looked natural. I passed it not without some emotion as the spot where we started our experiment in home-making which has been such a success." He noted that electric streetcars were now running in the old neighbourhood. "Further down Balmoral Street I did not place the last house we lived in. There is a house there, but it does not look like the one in which we froze."

There were other reminders that time had hurried by. During a Sunday walk with Macklin in St. John's Cathedral cemetery he noticed the tombstone of "a young man whom I thought was still in the land of the living: he has been dead for seven years."

Nevertheless, he was constantly reminded of how happy he was to be back in Winnipeg. "The day is a beautiful one," he wrote in a letter to Alice one day in late summer. "I had forgotten how incomparable Manitoba weather at its best can be." Everyone, he told Alice, was talking of a bumper crop, even the elevator boy at the *Free Press* office. "You see how rapidly I have turned Westerner again with my talk of crops and weather. I went to River Park to watch a ball game yesterday and enjoyed every minute of the weather: the game was pretty fair too."

He was annoyed at having to pay $50 for a frock coat and other formal accoutrements in order to attend a function at Government House, a luncheon for the visiting Duke and Duchess of York and Cornwall. "I shall have, after all my protestations, to get under a plug hat. I suppose I might as well face the fact that this position carries with it certain social obligations and so get into the swim—but no deeper than I have to." He was there at the station "in my war paint and plug hat" with a group of local Tory big-wigs when the royal train pulled in. He later got his first ticking-off from an outraged Laurier for using an editorial on the royal visit to take a sharp poke at the bumptious Lord Minto, the meddlesome Governor-General of Canada, who was regarded by

Jack—and Sifton—as a blunt instrument of British colonialism. The *Free Press*, on this occasion, spoke strongly for Winnipeg and the West and Laurier's protests were ignored. During a subsequent visit to Winnipeg by Lord Minto the city fathers honoured him by re-naming a street in what was then the red light district "Minto Street."

Jack was already planning his daily routine as editor of the *Free Press*. In a letter to Alice written in early September he laid out his plan of work. "I propose to work very assiduously from 9:00 A. M. to 1:00. Then home for lunch and a visit and back to the office between 3:00 and 4:00, then home for dinner at 6:00. While I do not expect to be in the office all the time," he continued, "I fancy the FP will never be long out of my mind. You do not know how pleased I am to be here," At this time he also began his lifelong custom of returning to the office for an hour or two after dinner. "I hereby invite you to come with me as often as you like," he told Alice.

It is unlikely that—with a houseful of young children—Alice ever took him up on his offer to go to the office with him in the evenings. Nevertheless, he frequently sought her advice and opinion on difficult issues. His long-time assistant, George Ferguson, in a memoir published in 1948, reported that "He considered his wife the best judge of the tone and temper of what appeared in the *Free Press*. Now and again they differed sharply on policy and when these rare divergences appeared there was no doubt whose view prevailed: it was his. But on matters of taste and feeling certainly, and perhaps in a wider range as well, Mrs. Dafoe's opinion was the most important in the world to him. More than once, something was ordered in or something was ordered out simply because 'Alice thinks it wise.'"

His first weeks on the job in 1901 were hectic, as he reported in a letter to Alice on 6 September: "We have had a busy time here since the news came of the shooting of President McKinley.

On a low estimate our telephone has been rung 250 times since then by persons wanting information. I kept the unfortunate Mr. Jeffers sitting right before the telephone and he was kept busy. The *Free Press* is a recognized bureau of information here and the telephone rings all night." Winnipeg had come a long way since 1865 when news of the assassination of President Abraham Lincoln had taken weeks to reach the settlement.

At the end of August he had gone out to Killarney for a visit with the family, his first sight of his mother and father in a decade, and had found them in mourning for his sister Edith's husband, Charles Fowler, who had recently died, leaving a young family. His parents had aged, especially his mother, and his sisters, he reported to Alice, looked older than expected. Hard work on the land was taking its toll, but otherwise the prospects were pleasing. The extended family was growing and prospering. A new generation of children was rising and on the land a bumper crop was predicted: "the greatest crop ever seen here," Jack noted.

Jack's brother Rance, who had returned from the East, was helping to draw in the oat crop, but still held fast to his old dream of becoming a newspaperman. Jack, who thought Rance would make an admirable farmer, finally promised him a try-out at the *Free Press*. The strong-willed Rance would spend all his working life at the newspaper.

Back in Winnipeg and counting the days before he left for Quebec to collect Alice and the children, Jack kept busy putting his new house in order; learning how to manage the hot air furnace, arranging the furniture and getting his books stowed away in bookcases, pausing now and again to browse through favourite volumes. On the 28th he paid his bill at the Leland, had his trunk sent over and slept, snug and warm, at 509 Spence for the first time. Three days later he was on the train for the East to collect the family at Hill Head and to meet Sifton in Ottawa to report on his first weeks at the *Free Press*.

It was a large party that set out for the West in early October, consisting of Jack and Alice, the six children and brother Rance's bride-to-be, Mary McLeod. It was a journey that Jack would often recall with a shudder in years to come. "The memory of that trip lingered in Dafoe's mind," George Ferguson would write, "and he often spoke of it, but not of his excitement at the beginning of a new editorial adventure, or of his return to a city that already had fond associations for him. What remained was mostly the memory of the train-sickness of his children and how he had torn the whole back out of his shirt to provide the necessary materials for the constant mopping up process that was needed. When he arrived in Winnipeg all that was left of that garment was the amount needed to hold the neckband and the equivalent of a dickey."

With the difficulties of family travel behind him, the editor was able to get down to his work in earnest, one of his first tasks being to launch total war against Manitoba Premier Rodmond Roblin and his Conservative government. Urged on by Sifton, the attack was conducted in the full glory and bombast of nineteenth-century political journalism at its most vigorous, with satirical onslaughts, outrageous revelations, harsh personal attacks and almost anything else that seemed likely to blacken the reputation of the political enemy. In a "Rome versus Carthage" battle that raged on to the end of the 1903 provincial election and beyond the attack was unrelenting, spilling over from the editorial columns onto the news pages. Members of the Roblin cabinet appeared in a "rogues gallery" lineup in the *Free Press*. The attorney-general, it was asserted, had instructed provincial magistrates to go easy on horse thieves, bootleggers, bawdy-house keepers and other miscreants if they agreed to support the Tories. "Voters," it was hinted, had been imported from Chicago to cast ballots on behalf of citizens who, although dead, were somehow still on the voters' lists. The Roblin forces fought back. The editor of the *Free Press* was sued for libel (the case was dismissed). Threats were exchanged.

For a time the editor carried a walking stick weighted with lead when he made his midnight walk home from the office. The Tory government won the 1903 election with an increased majority, Premier Roblin surviving the onslaught until 1915, resigning in that year over a scandal associated with the construction of the new legislative building.

The pressure to fight the battle against the Tories by any means possible short of murder receded considerably in 1905 when Sifton left the Laurier cabinet, remaining an MP, and residing, for the most part, in Toronto. His close ties with the *Free Press* editor would be maintained until his death in 1929. With editorial control of the paper more firmly in his hands, Jack was free to turn his attention to other issues that would be of particular interest to him in the years ahead. The questions of Canada's place in the greater world and its relationship with Britain and the Empire had been of importance to him since his earliest years in journalism and he now took up the battle anew. He was an outraged onlooker in 1903 when British negotiators, acting, ostensibly, on Canada's behalf, conceded to the Americans almost everything they had demanded in the Alaska Boundary dispute. In the years that followed Jack was to be an active participant in the struggle for full Canadian nationhood, frequently denounced as a traitor to the Motherland by Union Jack-waving empire boosters.

During his first years as editor Jack would seek out and hire outstanding journalists to add to the FP roster, one of the first being the remarkable E. Cora Hind, the oracle of wheat, who had the uncanny ability to stand in a field of ripening grain and predict to within a few bushels the probable yield at harvest time. Her crop reports and harvest predictions amazed the world. Miss Hind was soon joined by another formidable woman, Elizabeth Fulton Parker, who swept into the *Free Press* offices one morning in late 1903 to complain about the paper's coverage of literary events in the city. After a short conversation, the editor, impressed,

hired her to write a literary column that expanded into a daily cau-
serie in 1912, continuing until shortly before her death in 1940.
Both women reminded the editor of the impressive and forceful
women he and Alice had admired while reading and discussing
the plays of Ibsen years earlier, Miss Hind being a leading suffra-
gist and feminist, Mrs. Parker the founding secretary of the Alpine
Club of Canada. Newspapers were still largely a male preserve in
the early 1900s, but Jack had learned to accept talent where he
found it. He recalled his early association with Annette Parmelee
at the *Montreal Star* and he had first known the historian and
author Agnes Laut when she was an editorial writer at the *Free
Press* in the 1890s.

Remembering his own days as a young, ambitious newsman,
Jack was always on the lookout for youngsters of promise. When
the teenaged son of a friend from former days applied for a job at
the *Free Press* shortly before the First World War, Jack gave him a
trial, first as an office boy, then as a reporter. Grant Dexter would
become one of the greatest of Canadian political reporters and
a future editor of the *Free Press*. George Ferguson, a Canadian
Rhodes Scholar at Oxford in the early 1920s had been consid-
ering a job on the *Times*, but quickly accepted a counter-offer
from the *Free Press* after hearing the Winnipeg editor speak to a
group of students and dons at the Raleigh Club. Joining the *Free
Press* in 1924, he would, in time, become Jack's right hand and
his eventual successor. The editor's son Ted joined the paper as a
copy runner in the years before the First World War and would
eventually rise to the position of managing editor. Ted's younger
brother Jack was less fortunate. Returning from service in the First
World War, Jack, a keen athlete, was hired as a sportswriter while
his father was still travelling in Europe. Visiting the newsroom
upon his return, the editor was surprised to see his younger son
seated at a desk pecking away at a typewriter. "What are you doing here?" he asked. "I'm a sports writer," said young Jack. "No

you're not," said his father, "one son in the business is enough."
Jack moved on to a career in the grain business. The third son,
Van, solved the problem by going into public relations.

Jack's interest in literature never waned. His library grew
year by year. As he grew older he wrote no verse himself, but he
kept up to date with current poetry, absorbing Eliot, Yeats, E.J.
Pratt and others as they came along. There was always space on
the *Free Press* editorial page for poetry and at a time when few
literary magazines were available to print the works of young
Canadian poets many found space in the pages of the *Free Press*.
Book reviews remained a priority and he maintained friendships
with scholars and critics such as E.K. Brown. His old literary
friendships continued over the years. Archibald Lampman was
dead before 1900, but Bliss Carman, Duncan Campbell Scott and
others remained cronies and on visits to New York, Montreal,
Toronto and London Jack would often be missed by his journalist friends who did not know that he was tucked up in a book-
lined room somewhere "talking shop." It is interesting to note that
the 1941 "Canadian Number" of Harriet Munroe's celebrated
Chicago magazine *Poetry* is dedicated to "John W. Dafoe, Editor-
in-Chief of the *Winnipeg Free Press* and Architect of the Canadian
Future." This unusual dedication is not explained. Perhaps none
was required.

Throughout his years as editor Jack Dafoe would make merit-
based appointments a priority, often employing unusual methods
of recruitment, as in the case of a *Free Press* janitor who, working
on the overnight shift, took to leaving samples of his writing on
the editor's desk. At first the offerings were returned the following night with suggestions for improvement. In time, the janitor's
literary efforts, not bad to begin with, had become so much better
that he was given a writing job on the paper, eventually rising to
the journalistic front rank. Another was Thomas B. Roberton, a
Scottish immigrant who was working as a typesetter on another

newspaper when his exceptional ability as an essayist came to the attention of the editor of the *Free Press*. Roberton was offered a berth on the editorial page, eventually rising to the position of assistant editor. Another happy discovery was the amusing D.B. MacRae, "the only man I ever hired 'unsight unseen'; the letter I got from him from an Ontario town was irresistible." Jack never forgot his own beginnings at the *Montreal Star* in 1883, when he, an ambitious nobody, had been taken up and promoted by astute editors. He remembered, as well, his childhood on the farm at Combermere and his Grandfather Elcome's stories of the struggles of landless farm workers in Kent in the 1840s and 50s. Perhaps Jack remembered his Grandfather Elcome when he was asked to speak to a new generation of immigrants at J.S. Woodsworth's "People's Forum" in Winnipeg's North End.

The death, early in 1918, of Alice's sister Annette hit them both hard. Annette and her husband had suffered more than their fair share of misfortune over the years, culminating in the death of a son at the front in 1915. In a letter to Alice who was visiting her family in Ottawa at the time of Annette's death, Jack wrote: "When I recall her as a brilliant, handsome and ambitious girl, and think of what Fate did to her I feel a renewed sense of the tragi-comedy of human life. I owed Annette affection and grati- tude. Had I never known her I should in all probability never have met you. Even after 28 years of having you all to myself, I do not like to think that I might have passed you in the press of life and so gone companionless." Annette did not live to see two more of her children die in the Spanish Flu pandemic that reached North America late in 1918.

Jack made his first visit to his mother's homeland in 1906, continuing his journey to Paris and as far as Italy to cover meet- ings of the International Chamber of Commerce. Thereafter he became a frequent trans-Atlantic traveller—in spite of his suscep- tibility to seasickness—and a keen observer and well-informed commentator on world affairs. He was with the Canadian delegation to the Peace Conference at Paris in 1919 when Canada fought for and obtained the place it had earned at the peace table. He would become a die-hard champion of the League of Nations and a tireless advocate of collective security. He was a regular participant at Imperial Conferences, including the conference of 1930 that led to the Statute of Westminster which brought to Canada many of the powers that Jack had first called for long before when he was a young man starting out in journalism.

Always though the years he demonstrated his overarching concern for the development of Canada and, particularly, the affairs of the Canadian West. In 1911 he and Sifton would amicably agree to temporarily part company on the question of reciprocity with the United States, Sifton opposing the measure, the editor of the *Free Press*, convinced of the importance of free trade to the future of Western Canada, vigorously supporting it in the pages of Sifton's newspaper. Originally a "free trader" in the Liberal tradition, Sifton had gone sour on the matter as early as 1891, as he confided to Jack when his appointment was being negotiated in 1901. Sifton, in fact, was convinced that free trade would be bad for Canada, including the West, and he was sure, as he said in later years, that the Americans would never negotiate a free trade agreement that was not "jug-handled in their favour." Jack himself was a strong free trader, having imbibed the doctrine in his youth through the writings of Cobden, John Bright and other free trade apostles of the Manchester brotherhood.

In 1901 this difference of opinion between owner and editor hardly seemed to matter. Free trade was a faint cloud on the horizon at best. By early 1911, however, the storm was blowing and the sides were lining up. Sifton, no longer in the cabinet but still a force in the Liberal Party and an MP, became a leader in the anti-reciprocity forces, writing and speaking vigorously against the measure, predicting blue ruin and the possible end of Canadian independence should Laurier prevail. The *Free Press*, after a slow start, soon warmed to the task of supporting free trade, the editor feeling that it was his job to stand up for Western interests and to preserve the *Free Press* as a voice for Western concerns.

In the general election of September 1911 the Liberals went down to defeat and reciprocity became, for a time, a dead issue. The paper, however, was not downhearted. The debate had redefined the Canadian political landscape and reactivated the Liberal Party which had seemed headed into a decline. "We are thus certain," an FP editorial cheerfully stated, "to have henceforth in Canada a real Liberal and a real Tory party. We believe the change will operate to the public good. Parties with real policies and real principles, for which they will fight and face defeat, are factors of great value in the moral and material development of a nation. There is no need to regret that the truce between the conflicting economic ideas in Canada, which has persisted now for fifteen years, has come to a definite close." The Liberal Party, the *Free Press* editor felt, had been dying of hardening of the arteries. The debate, even if lost, had brought it back to life. Its greatest days—and the greatest days of the *Free Press*—were still ahead.

Canadian newspapers changed greatly during Jack's years as editor of the *Free Press*, as he noted in a letter to Sir Clifford Sifton marking the proprietor's retirement from the *Free Press* board in 1927, two years before Sifton's death. The newspaper, Jack observed, "in addition to discharging its original functions, is now a daily entertainer. But the original newspaper is still there and can be easily located under the comic cuts, the trashy fiction, and the advice to the lovelorn. I accept all these features as necessary; but I hold as firmly as ever that its has got to be a newspaper and an organ of public opinion too—that, in fact, if it isn't a good newspaper in addition to all these added functions it will find its foundations, not of rock but of sand. The vital element in a newspaper's life is prestige; and it can only be got from the legitimate news columns and from the editorial page. I think the most telling illustration of this is from our own experience. Nothing, in my opinion, has done so much to give this paper prestige at home, throughout Canada and outside of Canada as the apparently unconscious way in which we persisted in our advocacy of full nationhood for Canada in spite of all the influences, social, business financial and political which were brought to bear to pull us off. You and I did this in conjunction; I always knew that you were there behind me, even if you gave no sign. Even when the issue was in doubt our fighting attitude on the question was an asset, even if a few hundred Tories may have boycotted the paper—I doubt if the number really exceeded a score. When I was on the other side of the world two years ago I found that I didn't have to explain to the newspaper men or public men what the *Free Press* was; they knew about us. I don't think this was due to the excellence of our comic strips. My taking part in the symposium at Chicago—which I don't think did any harm to me or the *Free Press*—was, of course, the result of the knowledge of the university authorities that the *Free Press* was the most Canadian of Canadian papers." Jack then stated what he called "the cardinal quality of the *Free Press* editorial policy—having big views on big questions and fighting for them." That ideal kept the *Free Press* in the front rank of North American newspapers for much of the twentieth century.

The policy did not, as some have suggested, involve the paper in slavish support of the Liberal Party, right or wrong. During the First World War the *Free Press* would back Robert Borden's Union Government and involve itself fully in the great battle over conscription and in the 1920s it would make friends with liberal-leaning members of the Progressive Party, especially Thomas Crerar who became a bosom friend of the editor.

During the 1930s Jack was denounced as a "war-monger" when he persisted in attacking Nazi Germany and calling on

Canada to prepare to defend its freedom. When he denounced the Munich appeasement in a hard-hitting editorial entitled "What's the Cheering For?" many old friends and acquaintances cut him in the street and a large number of Manitobans cancelled their subscriptions to the *Free Press*. In response to complaints from the FP Circulation Department he intensified his jeremiad. Standing up for the League of Nations and writing day after day in support of collective security in the face of hostility—and, even worse, indifference—was a heartbreaking task in those years before the war resumed after a twenty-year intermission. Being out of step with a Liberal party led into Cloud-cuckoo-land by Mackenzie King and others who felt that Hitler was sound at heart and could be "talked around" wore on his nerves. He developed shingles and his asthma grew worse. He took to sleeping in a chair, propped up with pillows, waking in the night and reading or writing until he could sleep again. Alice watched and worried. In a letter to the family written from Ottawa in November 1938 she described a particularly disturbing public event: "Your Father had a rather trying ordeal. Sat at the head table at a League of Nations dinner and heard a man for whom he has an affectionate regard (Ernest Lapointe) make a speech in which he said all the things that your Father disbelieves. We were at opposite ends of the long table and I could only get a glimpse of him by leaning far forward. I was apprehensive of what the enforced restraint might do to him physically and at the worst passages I had visions of him getting to his feet and like Sampson pulling the edifice so queerly erected by Mr. L. and the Prime Minister down upon our heads. I waited for him anxiously after and found that he and Mrs. Norman Rogers had had a *good time* baiting Paul Martin who also had been a delegate to the Geneva Conference. Mr. Martin was astonished and said he had no idea that any one in Canada held such opinions. Poor Bob Inch came to your Dad after and said 'Now what do we do?' He had pleaded with your Father to speak too and give a little opposition to the policies that he feared would be advocated, but your Father refused. He does not think he should get into any controversies until his work with the Royal Commission is through. And that is right, I think. The P.M. did not speak at this meeting but was present and Monsieur Lapointe assured us that he was in agreement with him."

Jack's policy, in fact, was not to get mad and pull down the temple, but keep the arguments rolling in like waves, to achieve, by repetition and force, the wearing away of opposing positions. Whether it was freight rates or collective security, you kept slogging away. It was always better to be right than to be merely popular. "I know nothing that is better for a newspaper in the long run," he wrote in the last year of his life, "than that it should, when the occasion arises, face unpopularity in the advocacy of causes which it believes to be right. The resulting temporary loss is like the pruning of a vigorous plant in preparation for a greater growth. With this policy, to which Mr. Macklin and I subscribed, the proprietors of the *Free Press* were in thorough agreement. The *Free Press* must be the champion of the West's interests and the final judgments as to the nature of that advocacy left to the parties into whose hands the conduct of the paper had been given." It was a policy that few newspaper owners would subscribe to and probably had more to do with the *Free Press* editor's stature than it had to the proprietor's broadness of mind. Nevertheless, Jack was always ready to come to the defence of his employers. "There is a fairly general idea," he mused in later life, "that while the editor is a noble fellow desirous of serving the public interests, he is blocked in this purpose by the hard-faced men in the counting-rooms whose one idea is to make money. For over half a century I have held positions which brought me into daily contact with business managers and with proprietors, but I have never encountered the hard-faced, hard-fisted money-grubber. I don't think he exists outside of movieland and the realm of fiction."

J.W. Dafoe was editor of the *Free Press* for over forty years and he took part in all the battles of those difficult decades. He was in the thick of the fight over conscription during both world wars and in the struggle that saw the Empire evolve into the Commonwealth and Canada step into its place among the nations of the world. He travelled widely, attending international conferences and lecturing at public forums in Canada, the United States, Australia and Europe. He published books, including studies of Laurier and Clifford Sifton and his meditation on Canadian-American relations published under the title *Canada: An American Nation*. He became Chancellor of the University of Manitoba at a time when its fortunes were at a low ebb and for over a decade presided over its recovery. He declined opportunities to enter politics or take a seat in the Senate or assume an important diplomatic post, insisting always that the *Free Press* provided him with the best of all possible platforms. In his old age, when other contemporaries had already retired, he reluctantly accepted a position on the Royal Commission on Dominion-Provincial Relations, the Rowell-Sirois Commission, and the years of travel, intense discussion and sleepless nights pulled him down. At Christmas 1943 his family was alarmed at how weary he looked. As 1944 began it appeared that he might be living on borrowed time.

His oldest friends were already gone or were beginning to leave the stage. His friend the writer and publisher George Iles, first encountered in Montreal in the early 1880s and a regular provider of interesting books, good conversation and useful information over the years, had written from his home in New York in January, 1942, enclosing an appropriate gift book for an old companion who had already passed the allotted three score and ten. *The Inspiration of Old Age*, an anthology of prose and verse about growing old by such writers, ancient and modern, as Epictetus, Cicero, Francis Bacon, Joseph Addison, Walter Savage Landor, Matthew Arnold and Jack's particular favourite,

Ralph Waldo Emerson, was just the book to shorten the hours on cold, dark winter nights in Winnipeg when sleep would not come. George Iles himself was coming to the end of his journey. Inside the front cover Jack wrote in pencil: "His last book to me. He died July 1942 in his 90th year."

The Editor-in-Chief was at his desk at the *Free Press* office on Carlton Street on the day before he died, a Saturday, and had planned to finish an article at the card table in his bedroom on the Sunday morning, January 9, when an intense pain, which was at first attributed to appendicitis but was, in fact, an aneurysm, imposed his final deadline. He died in his doctor's car on the way to the hospital. He still had much to do, but that task would fall to others now. "The most inspiring of sights," he had told an audience of university students in 1923, "is not the young man starting forth in the morning amongst the plaudits of his friends, alive with hope and ambition, fired with generous desires, but the grey man at the end of the road who has outlived individual hope and fear and yet 'obeys the voice at eve obeyed at prime'—who has faith in mankind and in the future of the world and looks forward in the spirit to achievements that he will never see." Such thoughts can soften the sting of death.

But all that was far in the future and not to be considered. We live from day to day and let the future take care of itself. In the autumn of 1901 as he took up his new duties at the *Free Press* old age was only a faint shadow on a far horizon. In the first year of the new century, as his family settled happily into its new home in Winnipeg, Jack Dafoe looked around him and was amazed that he had at last landed in a place and time in which he could create a newspaper and help to create a country for a new age, making use of everything he had learned during the long, eventful years of his apprenticeship and looking forward to everything he would discover and experience in the uncounted years ahead. There was much to learn and his education would go on until the day he died. The adventure had only just begun under the broad and ever-changing prairie sky. He was 35 years old. He had travelled far, from childhood to maturity, with his dreams for Canada, all that it was, all that it could become, foremost in his mind. His search for a better Canada would consume his remaining years. As the twentieth century began he joyfully took up his new and heavier burden and resumed his pilgrimage.

INDEX